THE
NEW GUIDE
TO
MUSHROOMS

THE NEW GUIDE TO MUSHROOMS

THE ULTIMATE GUIDE TO IDENTIFYING, PICKING AND USING MUSHROOMS

PETER JORDAN

Sebastian Kelly

This edition published in 1997 by
Sebastian Kelly
2 Rectory Road
Oxford OX4 1BW

© Anness Publishing Limited 1995, 1996

Produced by Anness Publishing Limited

ISBN 1 901688 26 7

A CIP catalogue record for this book is available
from the British Library

Publisher: Joanna Lorenz
Project Editor: Clare Nicholson
Designer: Michael Morey
Illustrator: Adam Abel
Indexer: Alex Corrin

This book was previously published as part of a larger compendium,
The Ultimate Mushroom Book

Printed in Singapore by Star Standard Industries Pte. Ltd.

1 3 5 7 9 10 8 6 4 2

CONTENTS

Introduction

FOREWORD

I was introduced to wild mushrooms by my grandfather who was a farmer in Norfolk, England. From the age of four I would go out in the fields with him to collect not only what he described as field mushrooms, but also some weird and wonderful looking toadstools which I thought were poisonous – they certainly looked menacing to a child. However, he taught me one very good lesson: so long as you can identify absolutely accurately what you are picking you will be safe. From these early beginnings developed a lifetime's interest in wild mushrooms.

The excitement of walking along a woodland path in the autumn, and finding in front of you two or three perfectly formed ceps is wonderful. During fifty years as a mushroom hunter, I have graduated from the relatively common horse and field mushrooms to the more exotic chanterelles and ceps. I am still excited when I find the first morels of the spring, or the year's first patch of chanterelles hidden in the leaf litter; of course, the more elusive the mushroom, like the horn of plenty or the winter chanterelle, the greater the excitement. Imagine the ultimate triumph of finding your first truffle – of beating the pigs and squirrels to them! But, as well as providing excitement and good eating, mushrooms can be dangerous; correct identification is the key to successful mushroom collecting.

The fruits, nuts and mushrooms of autumn are obvious and most are easy to spot. But have you ever realized that the winter, spring and summer can be as productive – at least as far as mushrooms are concerned? Mushrooms are one of the few wild treasures available nearly all the year round. Even on a crisp winter's day you can find a bouquet of silver-grey oyster mushrooms or the wonderful velvet shank growing out of a tree stump and it is so much more satisfying to pick them like this than from a supermarket shelf. Because, of course, the excitement of finding the mushrooms is closely followed by the satisfaction of cooking them within hours if not minutes of their harvest.

Identifying mushrooms, utterly essential though it is, can be frustrating if you have to wade through hundreds of illustrations, many of which look the same. This book is designed to make that task easier. It illustrates the best of the edible mushrooms, and so will help you pick your way wisely through the year's mushrooms, alerting you not only to a season's treasures, but also to the poisonous lookalikes and really deadly fungi that all too often grow alongside innocent and delicious mushrooms. The section that deals with the poisonous species will help identification and give the faint-hearted confidence to take their finds back to the kitchen. But do follow the advice given in this guide carefully. If clear identification is not possible from this book, consult others – the bibliography lists some of the best. And remember that the best advice of all is: if in doubt do not collect a mushroom and never, ever, eat anything you cannot identify with certainty.

Peter Jordan

WHAT ARE MUSHROOMS?

The terms mushrooms, toadstools and fungi (singular fungus) are often used loosely and interchangeably. However, this can be misleading.

The fungi are a very large group of organisms and include moulds, yeasts, mushrooms and toadstools. None of these organisms contain the green pigment chlorophyll, so they cannot make their own food by the process known as photosynthesis. So, although you may encounter some mushrooms with a distinctly greenish tinge, none are green in the way that a tree or a flowering plant is.

Mushrooms are usually defined as the edible, spore-producing bodies of some fungi. In contrast, the term toadstool is commonly applied to the spore-producing bodies of those fungi that are not only inedible but may also be highly dangerous. From this you will realize that while the terms fungus and fungi have a very precise scientific meaning, mushroom and toadstool do not. In this book mushroom is used whether, or not, the fruit body of that particular fungus is edible. It is used to cover a large number of different types of fungi such as mushrooms, boletes, bracket fungi, puff balls and cap fungi.

Ascomycetes

The cup fungi circle shows details of the spore-bearing surface.

Basidiomycetes

The gilled mushroom circle shows the enlargement of the gill edge.

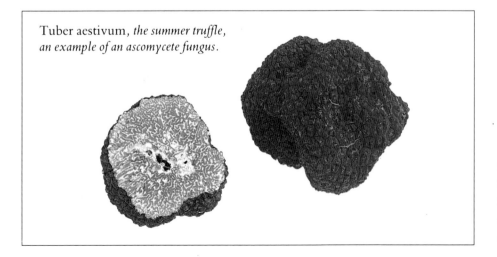

Tuber aestivum, *the summer truffle, an example of an ascomycete fungus.*

The fungi in this book divide into two main groups: the Ascomycetes and the Basidiomycetes. The Ascomycetes produce spores that are spread by the wind. Among this group are many of the cup fungi, including the common morel and *Gyromitra esculenta*. Because the wind spreads the spore of many of these mushrooms, it is worth remembering when you find some morels, for example, to check downwind and you will almost certainly find some more.

The second group, and by far the largest as far as the collector is concerned, is the Basidiomycetes, which includes the large and well-known Agaric and Boletus families. These two families, in fact, form sub-divisions within the group.

A mushroom of the Agaric type is illustrated here with the various parts clearly identified. This is a gilled mushroom and sometimes grows from an egg-shaped volval bag. Care must be taken when dealing with any mushroom that grows from a volval bag, because this is how the *Amanitas*, the most deadly of all mushroom species, grow.

Parts of the Agaric-type fungi

The universal veil encloses the whole mushroom and the partial veil covers the gills. As the mushroom grows the universal veil ruptures to leave a volva and fragments on the cap, and the partial veil ruptures to leave a ring on the stem.

Parts of the Boletus-type fungi

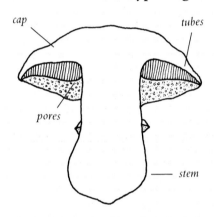

A second sub-division is the Boletes. Instead of having gills, mushrooms in this group have tubes and pores which vary widely in colour. Boletes, like Agarics, are fleshy and decay readily. This separates them from the Polypores. It is important to note their colour because this can be a clear indicator of the mushrooms you have found. The cep is the best-known member of this group.

A third group of fungi illustrated in this book is Aphyllophorales. This group includes the polypores and chanterelles and a number of other mushrooms that have irregular shapes. A number of fungi fall into this group, for example, the hedgehog fungus, which, instead of gills, has tiny spines from which it gets its name. Another member of the group is the cauliflower fungus. It may look odd, but it is a wonderful find from a culinary point of view. Other unusual types are the beefsteak fungus and the sulphur polypore or chicken of the woods. Both are excellent for cooking as well as being quite spectacular when you encounter them in the wild.

Examples of the two types of fungi which form sub-divisions of the Basidiomycetes. The horse mushroom (above) and the cep (right).

Cauliflower fungus is an example of the third major group of fungi, the Aphyllophorates.

THE DIFFERENT PARTS OF MUSHROOMS

When collecting wild mushrooms it is important to consider carefully what it is that you are collecting. The mushroom itself can be divided into various parts. From both the collecting and culinary points of view the cap or fruit body is the most important part. The shape, size and colour of the cap can show tremendous variation within a species, which is one of the reasons why mushrooms are so difficult to identify accurately. It is also important to note whether the cap has gills or pores, what the colours of these are and whether they are crowded or open.

Stems can also vary considerbly and they, too, can often be an important indicator of precisely which mushroom you have discovered. Does the stem have a veil or not? The base of the stem is a vital means of identification, particularly if you have any doubts about the specimens you have found. If you are not sure what it is, carefully dig out the mushroom so that you can see the base of the stem. If there is any sign of a volval bag have nothing more to do with the mushroom. Incidentally, whatever the mushroom that you are digging up proves to be, do be careful not to do too much damage to the mycelial threads that connect it to the rest of the underground part of the fungus.

The colour of the mushroom's flesh is another important means of identification. Not only should you look at the whole mushroom, you should also cut it through in cross-section. Some important details, such as whether the stem is hollow, can of course, only be seen in cross-section.

In some species the stems change colour quite dramatically when they are cut. Take note of any such changes, because they can be a reliable identification feature in certain types of mushroom.

Spore prints are also a good means of identifying mushrooms and are very easy to do. Take a cap or fruit body of a mature specimen of a mushroom and place it on black or white paper on top of a container, so that air can circulate around it. Leave in a warm place for up to three days so the mushroom sheds all its spores and you will have a very clear spore print. If you do not know what colour the spore will be, put down a piece of black paper and overlay part of it with white paper. Then place the cap so that it is half on the black paper and half on the white.

Examples of different shapes of stems

LEFT *To take a spore print you will need a mature specimen, white, or black and white paper and a container to place it on.*

LEFT BELOW *Leave the mushroom in a warm place for a few days.*

LEFT BOTTOM *Do not use just black paper because it will not show up if the spore print is a dark colour.*

BELOW *Taking a spore print is a very reliable way of making an accurate identification.*

WHERE TO COLLECT MUSHROOMS

Always take care when you are out mushroom collecting that you do not trespass. Always get the permission of the landowner before you go on to any land that is not open to the public. When you are mushroom collecting be careful of the surrounding countryside and its animals, otherwise not only will you soon get a bad reputation, but you will give other collectors a similar reputation whether they deserve it or not.

Most people limit their mushroom hunting to meadows, but these have suffered from being over enriched with nitrates, which have denuded many previously good mushroom-hunting territories. If you want to find meadowland mushrooms it is best to examine those meadows and marshes that have been treated with natural organic fertilizers and not nitrates. But why restrict yourself to meadowland species when eighty per cent of fungi grow in association with trees? Woods, forests and copses are the places where you should really be looking for mushrooms, but only, of course, once you have established you will not be trespassing.

Established woods and forests containing a wide variety of species provide the very best places for mushroom collecting and it is in such areas that the vast majority of species are to be found. Many of these fungi have a symbiotic relationship with trees and their roots, with some fungi growing only with a particular species of tree, while other fungi can be found in association with a number of different trees. For example, many boletes grow only with one type of tree such as the species of *Suillus* which only grow with conifers, or the species of *Leccinum* which are very specific: *Leccinum versipelle* grows with birch and *L. aurantiacum* with aspen. Chanterelles on the other hand can effectively grow with birch,

pine, oaks or even beech trees.

Soil type is also important. Although many trees grow on a variety of soils, you will find that some fungi will only grow with a particular tree on a particular soil, rather than across the whole range of soils on which the tree grows. For example the bay boletus grows under beech trees or under conifers on acid soils, and the panther cap grows under beech trees on chalk.

ABOVE *The early morning is prime mushroom hunting time.*

OPPOSITE *Do not restrict your mushroom hunting to meadows and woodlands: marshes and heathland can be surprisingly productive too.*

LEFT *Many mushrooms grow in rings, some of which reach several metres wide.*

WHEN TO COLLECT MUSHROOMS

Most people associate mushrooms with the autumn, but, in fact, they grow throughout the year.

The spring brings morels and the St George's mushroom *Calocybe gambosa*. The fairy ring champignon, *Marasmius oreades*, also appears quite early in the year. The first of the summer mushrooms is usually the field mushroom, *Agaricus campestris*. Another mushroom to appear fairly early in summer is the chicken of the woods, *Laetiporus sulphureus*, indeed it often catches collectors unawares with its early appearance. When, or indeed if, there is a spell of hot weather, there is usually little to be found, but these conditions are, nevertheless, important, because they help the mushrooms' underground mycelial threads to mature before the autumn's great burst of growth. If the weather is mild, the autumn can extend into early winter. The first touches of frost may herald

the coming of winter, but they can often bring exciting finds of both the field blewit, *Lepista saeva*, and the wood blewit, *Lepista nuda*. Both these species will continue until the weather turns quite frosty.

When winter takes hold, most

people give up and just look forward to the next mushroom season. But don't be fooled: on mild winter days go out searching and you will be surprised at what you find. Oyster mushrooms, *Pleurotus ostreatus*, will continue to grow almost right through the winter, together with the Jew's ear, *Auricularia auricula-judaea*, and the velvet shank, *Flammulina velutipes*. Finding these can make a cold winter walk tremendously exciting, and shows that even in the depth of winter you can enjoy a dish with ingredients freshly picked from fields and woods.

The mushroom collector's year never ends and even when you're not actually hunting, always be on the look-out for new spots. Use winter walks to examine pastures and woodlands that you have not been to before, to see if they give any clues as to what they are likely to produce when spring comes again.

It may seem surprising, but time of day is most important to the mushroom collector. This is because mushrooms grow almost exclusively

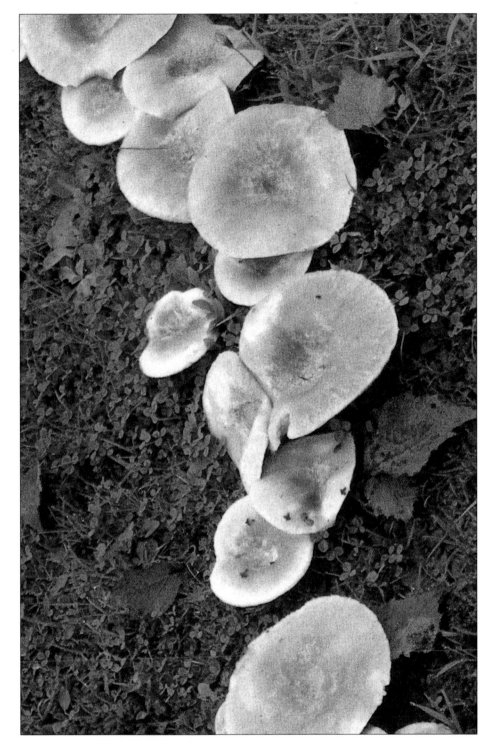

during the hours of darkness. As a result, the best specimens are picked when they are fresh in the early morning before the rising temperature of the day has brought out the flies to lay their eggs, so giving rise to maggot infestation, or the animals of the woods and fields have had their pickings of the overnight growth, which can be quite amazing in its quantity.

It is also worth revisiting a place you have picked after two or three days, because the mushrooms will usually have regrown. Ceps are known to regrow to a weight of ¾ kilo (1¾ lb) within two or three days of the first growth having been picked – an enormous rate of growth by any standard.

It is useful to keep a diary of what you find, when and where you found it, and what the climatic conditions were, as this will give you a key to subsequent seasons and help you develop a knowledge and understanding of your local area. Noting climatic conditions is also interesting as well as useful. Good fungal growth needs periods of damp, but also periods of dry and cold, as the mycelial threads seem to benefit from a degree of stratification which, in turn, gives rise to better fruiting, and thus to better collecting.

OPPOSITE ABOVE *Chicken of the woods grows from late spring to early autumn.*

OPPOSITE BELOW *Oyster mushrooms continue to grow through the winter.*

ABOVE *The poisonous* Clitocybe rivulosa *appears in summer and autumn.*

LEFT *Wood Blewits.*

HOW TO COLLECT MUSHROOMS

Very little equipment is needed for mushroom collecting. Tough outdoor clothes and a strong pair of boots are essential and you should make sure that your jacket or anorak has a pocket large enough to carry a small field guide. It is not an exaggeration: some mushrooms are just too dangerous to take home. You may find a wide-brimmed hat useful to wear in the autumn, as the days shorten and the sun is low. It is easier to spot those interesting little humps and bumps that could well prove to be an exciting find if you are not having to shade your eyes with your hand all the time.

One or two baskets are, of course, essential. They should be light, easy to carry and not too open in weave.

A sharp knife and brush are also important, the knife to cut the mushroom's stem through cleanly and the brush to remove obvious dirt and debris such as pine needles and leaf litter. Cleaning your specimens as you pick them will mean there is less to do when you get home. Several polythene bags or disposable gloves are also essential items to take

OPPOSITE
Results of a successful morning's mushroom collecting.

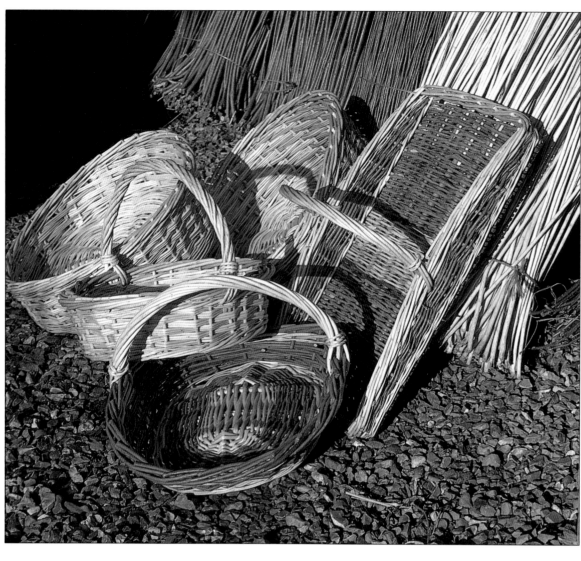

RIGHT *A selection of hand-made baskets.*

with you. You can put these over your hands when handling any specimens about which you are doubtful. Don't forget to throw them away after you have used them. A packet of tissues or a cloth will also be useful as your hands can get quite dirty. You will also need them to clean your knife, as you should clean it each time you use it.

The final item of equipment is a good strong stick or thumb-stick. You can use it to part bracken and undergrowth to see if any mushrooms are hidden there. It will be handy to turn over any specimens you may not wish to touch, as well as being useful as a tool to dig out specimens so that you can check if they have volval bags or not.

When you find a specimen that you want to collect, it is best to cut

BELOW *A good knife is an essential part of any mushroom collector's equipment. Two of the knives double up as a brush as well.*

through its stem rather than dig it up. While it is possible to use the stems of mushrooms such as ceps and chanterelles, there is a danger of disturbing the mycelial threads if the entire mushroom is removed from the ground. The only possible exception to this rule is if you are confronted by what you think may be a poisonous mushroom. Then dig it up with your stick, being careful not to damage it. If there is anything that looks even remotely like a volval bag at the base of the stem, leave the whole specimen very well alone.

Having cut through the mushroom's stem, wipe or brush clean the mushroom before putting it in your basket. As the basket starts to fill up, a layer of bracken fronds will prevent the bottom mushrooms from becoming damaged.

STORING MUSHROOMS

There are certain times of the year when mushrooms grow in great profusion. It is important, therefore, to find ways to preserve this abundance for those times when few mushrooms grow. Preserving food is as old as time itself and long before refrigerators, salting and drying were used as methods of preservation. There are many different ways to store mushrooms and some species are more suited to a certain type of preservation than others. Informa-

laying them on muslin trays in the sun can be quite sufficient. In cooler, less sunny regions, mushrooms can be dried on open trays in a warmstore, airing cupboard and on window ledges. It is important to remember that the mushrooms must be dried thoroughly, which may take several days and while drying is in progress an intense mushroomy smell will pervade wherever you are drying them.

In recent years, fruit dryers and drying machines have become avail-

tant to remember, however, that mushrooms such as morels could well have creepy-crawlies hiding inside so partially dry them somewhere before hanging them in your kitchen. This will prevent any wildlife dropping into your food. When the mushrooms are dry, carefully lay them on a sheet and pick the individual specimens over before placing them in airtight containers for storage. Don't waste any powder that may remain on the sheet, it can be

tion as to the most suitable method for each species is given in the relevant entry.

Whatever method of storage you are going to use, it is important to select the very best of the mushrooms you have collected. Do be careful to make sure that they are completely free of maggots and other insects because there is nothing worse when reconstituting dried mushrooms to find you have maggots floating on the top of the water in which they are being reconstituted. Also make sure there are no twigs, leaves or other debris among them.

Drying preserves the flavour and colour quite well, although unfortunately it often destroys the shape of the mushroom. There are several methods of drying. In warmer climates, slicing the mushrooms and

able. Some can take up to ten trays and are capable of drying a large quantity of wild mushrooms very effectively over several hours. The advantage of this is that it prevents the whole house smelling of mushrooms for days afterwards, and you can also be totally confident that your dried mushrooms are completely free of moisture. With this accelerated form of drying it is possible to dry even shaggy ink caps, so long as you use very young specimens. Ordinary drying methods are much too slow and they would collapse into an inky mess and probably ruin any other mushrooms you were drying with them.

Another effective way of drying mushrooms is to thread them with a needle and cotton and hang them up in strings in the kitchen. It is impor-

stored separately and used to flavour soups and stews.

Dried mushrooms can be used straight in soups and stews, but for other dishes it is best to reconstitute them in lukewarm water for around twenty minutes. Do not use boiling water as this will impair the final flavour. The water in which they have been reconstituted can be used as stock or to make gravy, but, before you do so, pour it through a sieve to remove any extraneous matter or grit that might have been contained within the mushrooms.

An alternative to drying, is freezing. Perhaps surprisingly, this is not a very good method of preserving mushrooms. For best results, make up the mushroom dishes and then freeze the finished dish or make up mushroom butter. To do this, slice

RIGHT *Mushrooms that have been dried and preserved for later use.*

OPPOSITE FAR LEFT AND MIDDLE *It is essential to brush and wipe clean mushrooms before they are dried or stored.*

OPPOSITE NEAR RIGHT *A mushroom drier.*

your mushrooms, add them to melted butter and freeze the result. Preserved like this you have the mushrooms and the butter for use with sauces, to flavour various dishes and to add to your meat or fish dishes as a topping.

Salting is one of the oldest methods of preserving food. It works extremely well for mushrooms. The most important thing to remember is to have clean, fresh mushrooms. The quantities required are one part salt to three parts mushrooms. It is important to layer the mushrooms and salt alternately, and make sure the final layer of mushrooms is completely covered with salt. Use containers that the salt will not corrode. Although a sterilized jar is best, you could also use polythene ice-cream containers. When preserving mush-

rooms in this way you will eventually have a lot of seasoned juice and you will not need to use salt in any dish you make using salted mushrooms.

Mushrooms can be pickled in either oil or good vinegar. It is most important when using this method to clean the mushrooms well and then blanch them. If you are pickling them with vinegar, remember that the better the vinegar, the better the results will be, so it is not worth putting good mushrooms in inferior vinegar. The same applies if you are pickling mushrooms in oil. It is also a good idea to put peppercorns and half a dozen cloves of garlic into each jar, together with two or three bay leaves. Make sure the containers you use have a good seal, and when they are filled, seal tightly.

Once the seals have been broken, use the contents fairly quickly. And it is a good idea to keep the container in the fridge while you are doing so. Even when you have finished the mushrooms, the oil or vinegar in which they have been stored will make a wonderful dressing. If you preserve mushrooms by pickling, you must remember to sterilize everything you use. You can do this by immersing all your utensils in boiling water, or by using a sterilizing solution. Boiling water is probably best as there is always a danger that the sterilizing solution might affect the taste of the mushrooms. Remember, too, to keep a watchful eye on your pickled mushrooms for any sign of mouldiness. If there is, discard the top few mushrooms and use the rest fairly quickly.

Edible Mushrooms

INTRODUCTION

This section illustrates and describes the best of the edible mushrooms that grow in our fields and woods. There are in fact over a thousand edible species and but only a small proportion of these are prized for their flavour and texture, and although personal taste will vary many consider the finest to include the cep *Boletus edulis*, bay boletus *Boletus badius*, morels *Morchella elata* and *esculenta*, chanterelle *Cantherellus cibarius* and chicken of the woods *Laetiporus sulphureus*. To enable identification each entry has a description of the mushroom in question, information on its habitat and season of growth, as well as hints on storage and cooking preparation for when you return home.

As you learn about mushrooms you will become more respectful of the rules of identification. No mushroom looks exactly like another, and sometimes the differences are great within the same species. Many species have poisonous lookalikes, which are also mentioned here. Take particular care with such mushrooms. It is also essential that you never pick immature specimens, because only with mature specimens can you be sure of an accurate identification.

Mushrooms are quite rich and even edible ones can cause stomach upsets. Some people seem more prone to these than others, so be careful if you are serving a mushroom dish to guests.

Although some mushrooms can be eaten raw, others must be cooked first. Among this group are honey fungus *Armillaria mellea*, wood blewit *Lepista nuda*, field blewit *Lepista saeva*, and the morels *Morchella elata* and *esculenta*. These all contain a small amount of poison which is removed by cooking.

One of the best ways to learn about mushrooms is to go on a foray led by an expert. Not only will you have the chance to question the expert about the location, type and size of the various mushrooms·that you find, but, at the end of the foray, you will have a chance to examine what everybody else has found and have them identified by the expert. In this way you will have an opportunity to see far more species than you would if you had just gone out collecting on your own.

Forays are run by many organizations, including mycological societies, local naturalists trusts and local experts who organize them on an ad-hoc basis. Details of forays can usually be found in your local library and they may also be advertised in the local paper.

Enjoy your mushroom collecting, but don't take any risks with mushrooms you cannot identify.

PREVIOUS PAGE *Beefsteak fungus,* Fistulina hepatica. *Although these mushrooms are usually found at the base of tree trunks they can grow high up on the branches.*

LEFT *Field blewit,* Lepista saeva.

OPPOSITE *Amethyst's deceiver,* Laccaria amethystea, *is a tasty mushroom that has a long season from late summer to early winter.*

Agaricus arvensis
HORSE MUSHROOM

This is one of the larger varieties of mushroom. It is quite meaty in texture and has a very distinctive aniseed smell. Horse mushrooms are best picked when they are young because not only are they soon attacked by maggots, but also the flesh becomes dark brown with age and will turn any cooked dish muddy brown in colour.

mature gills
turn dark brown,
immature gills are pinkish

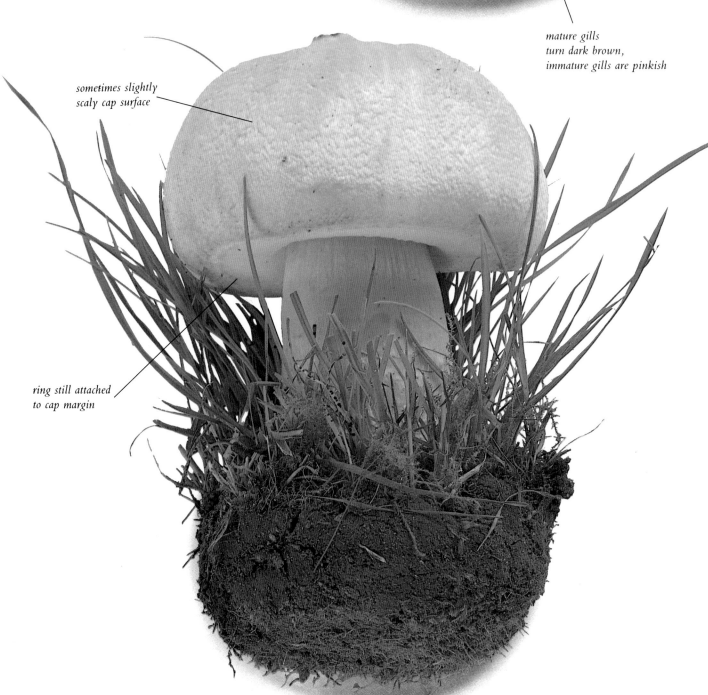

sometimes slightly
scaly cap surface

ring still attached
to cap margin

These mushrooms tend to come up in the same fields year after year, so having once found a good growth keep watching in future years.

The horse mushroom often has yellowish markings on the cap. When you find one like this, check it particularly carefully to ensure that it is not, in fact, the yellow stainer, *Agaricus xanthodermus*, which will make you very ill if you eat it. This mushroom is dealt with in detail in the section on poisonous mushrooms so you can compare the two. Unlike the yellow stainer, the horse mushroom does not colour when pressed or cut; the yellow colouring of the cap is its natural colour.

IDENTIFICATION

The cap can be from 10–25 cm (4–9¾ in) across. It is domed at first, but eventually expands to a fully convex shape. It is white but yellows with age. The stem is 8–10 cm (3–4 in) and has a large double ring. It may become hollow with age. The gills, which are white at first, turn a delicate pink and eventually dark brown in mature specimens. The flesh is thick and white but darkens with age and can become a little woolly lower down the stem. It has a distinct smell of aniseed. The spore print is dark brown.

HABITAT AND SEASON

Horse mushrooms favour grassland and pasture, particularly, as the name suggests, that where cattle or horses have grazed. Chalk meadows are often good places to look. The season is from midsummer to quite late autumn and they often grow in quite large rings.

STORAGE

These mushrooms dry well, but it is important to check thoroughly that they are maggot free. Slice and then dry either with open driers or with an electric drier.

PREPARATION AND COOKING HINTS

These mushrooms make wonderful meals, provided, of course, that they are not infested with maggots. Remember, too, if you are using older specimens when the flesh has turned dark brown, that they will change the colour of your dish.

ABOVE *The yellow stainer.*

ABOVE LEFT *The horse mushroom prefers open meadows and woodland edges.*

BELOW *The mature cap may turn brassy yellow with age or when wet.*

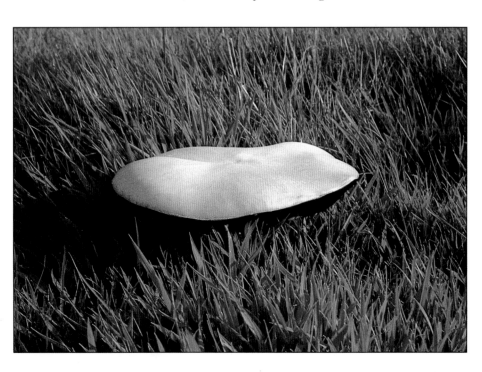

Agaricus augustus
THE PRINCE

The prince is a good mushroom to find, not only does it look attractive, it also has a lovely flavour and makes excellent eating. These mushrooms tend to grow in deciduous and coniferous woodland, and in clumps rather than rings.

IDENTIFICATION

The cap is 10–25 cm (4–9¾ in) across. Button-shaped at first, it opens to a convex form and is often irregular in shape. It is light brown in colour and has clearly marked rings of brown fibrous scales joining in the centre. The stem is 10–20 cm (4–7¾ in), off-white with small scales and a large floppy ring. The gills are off-white at first, turning dark brown with age. The flesh is thick, white and smells mushroomy. The spore print is brown.

HABITAT AND SEASON

The prince grows mainly in coniferous and deciduous woods, often in clumps. The season is late summer to late autumn.

STORAGE

As these mushrooms grow fairly large, make sure you have good specimens before slicing and drying them in the usual way. This is a good mushroom to store for winter use as it has an intensity of flavour which will enhance any mushroom dish.

PREPARATION AND COOKING HINTS

A nice mushroom that needs very little preparation. The stem tends to be quite fibrous, so is best discarded. The cap does not need peeling, just wipe lightly with a damp cloth before slicing. The prince makes an extremely good addition to omelettes, but is also nice on its own.

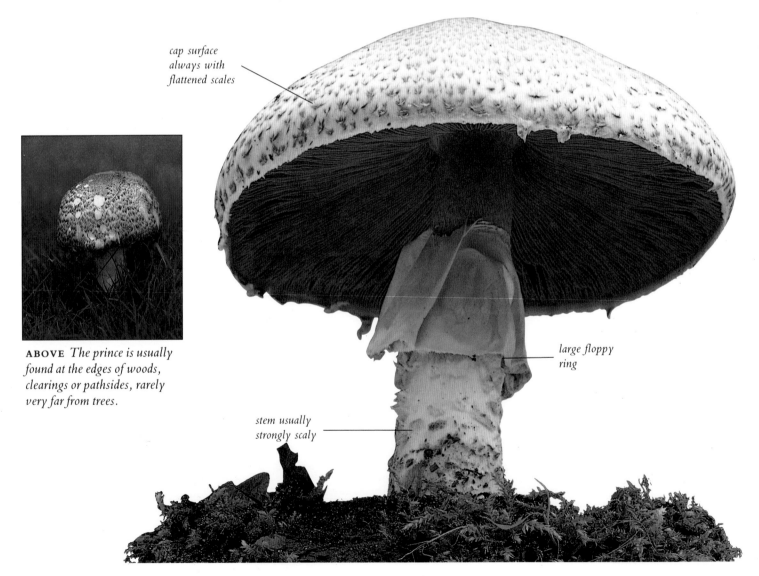

cap surface always with flattened scales

ABOVE *The prince is usually found at the edges of woods, clearings or pathsides, rarely very far from trees.*

large floppy ring

stem usually strongly scaly

Agaricus bisporus

Agaricus bisporus smells and tastes very similar to the field mushroom. It is believed to be the species from which most of the cultivated varieties come. It can grow in quite large quantities and is mostly found on wasteground and compost heaps. It is quite common.

IDENTIFICATION
The cap is 5–10 cm (2–4 in) across, button-shaped before opening almost flat. It is whitish to mid-brown in colour with flaky scales. The stem is 3–5 cm (1¼–2 in) and white, with a distinct ring below the cap. It has pink gills which become darker with age. The flesh is white, bruising slightly reddish and it has a distinct mushroomy smell. The spore print is brown.

ABOVE AND BELOW Agaricus bisporus *is the species that cultivated varieties come from. The button, cup and flat mushrooms, that are widely available, are the different stages of growth of this mushroom.*

HABITAT AND SEASON
It grows on compost heaps, in garden waste and beside roads, occasionally on the edges of hedges and small plantations, but very rarely in grass. The season is quite early in the spring through to late autumn.

STORAGE
This mushroom tends to be quite small and dries well, either whole or cut. It is full of flavour.

PREPARATION AND COOKING HINTS
Because this mushroom often grows on compost heaps or in rough ground, it is best to wipe the cap very thoroughly, cutting off the bottom of the stem and slicing through.

Agaricus campestris

FIELD MUSHROOM

The field mushroom is probably the best known of all wild mushrooms. Years ago fields were often carpeted with these small white mushrooms, but due to changes in farming technology and the greater use of herbicides, pesticides and, particularly, nitrates, many of the wonderful pastures where field mushrooms grew have disappeared. If you are lucky enough to have some old meadows and pasture near you, keep an eye open for a wonderful feast that can come at any time from quite early in the summer through to autumn. These mushrooms are best picked early in the morning, not only to beat other mushroom collectors, but also to ensure that they have not yet been attacked by maggots.

IDENTIFICATION

The cap is 3–12 cm (1¼–4¾ in) across. It retains its dome shape for some time before opening out fully. It is silky white, ageing to light brown. The stem is 3–10 cm (1¼–4 in),

*gills are
pink when
young*

*ring is fragile
and often missing*

LEFT *An
example of a
typical cultivated
edible* Agaricus
species.

white, tapering to the base, and has a thin ring which is often torn away. Even in unopened field mushrooms the gills are deep pink, an excellent identification feature. The white flesh bruises slightly pink. It has a pleasant smell. The spore print is brown.

HABITAT AND SEASON

Field mushrooms grow in mature pasture and often favour chalky soils. They can grow any time from early summer through to late autumn.

STORAGE

An excellent mushroom for storing dried as it retains its flavour extremely well. The smaller specimens can be threaded on string and dried whole, but larger ones should be sliced.

PREPARATION AND COOKING HINTS

These do not need peeling, a wipe with a damp cloth is sufficient, but do check them carefully to make sure there is no maggot infestation. The best way to do this is to trim the stem carefully and slice through the centre – any maggots will then be easy to see. The older specimens are best used for ketchup, sauces and stews, as these give a quite intense, dark brown colour to the dish. Young specimens can be used as you like. They are delicious for breakfast with bacon and eggs.

Agaricus macrosporus

This is quite a common autumn mushroom. It grows in rings and is extremely good to eat. Some care over identification is necessary, because it can look like the poisonous yellow stainer. However, the shape of the cap and, in particular, the smell are reliable aids to ensuring you have the right mushroom.

IDENTIFICATION
The domed cap is 8–10 (3–4 in) across. It is off-white with light brown scales. The scaly stem is 5–10 cm (2–4 in) long, off-white and quite thick, with a slightly pointed base. The gills are pale pink at first, turning darker brown with age. The flesh is white and has a fairly distinct smell of almonds. The spore print is brown.

HABITAT AND SEASON
Grows in rings in mature pastures that have not been treated with chemicals. The season is from late summer to autumn.

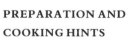

RIGHT *Often very large, the white cap may develop fine scales on the surface, as here.*

STORAGE
This mushroom is very good to eat. It is best dried for storage, but specimens can be quite large so it is important to slice them first.

PREPARATION AND COOKING HINTS
Clean the stem carefully and brush the cap: peeling is usually unnecessary. Check your specimens carefully, especially the larger ones, which may have become maggot infested.

thick ring with scaly underside

gills free from the stem

Agaricus silvaticus

This is a mushroom of mainly coniferous woodland, which grows in the same places year after year. It is also extremely good to eat.

IDENTIFICATION
The cap is 5–10 cm (2–4 in) across, convex and covered with brown scales which give it an overall broken pattern. The stem is 5–8 cm (2–3 in), whitish, but striated with brown markings; it has a brown ring. The gills are pale cream at first but turn quite red with age. The flesh is white and stains bright red when cut at the base or lengthways. It has very little smell. The spore print is brown.

HABITAT AND SEASON
The usual habitat is coniferous woods and the season is from early summer to late autumn.

STORAGE
This mushroom has quite an intense flavour. It is best dried, but as it is often large, it should be sliced first.

PREPARATION AND COOKING HINTS
Because this mushroom grows mainly in coniferous woods, the top will need brushing and any pine needles removing. Cut off the lower portion of the stem and slice. It will give a wonderful flavour to your dishes. It is also good on its own, lightly fried with a little butter and basil, and served on toast.

ring with small scales on underside

scaly cap surface scratches red

Agaricus silvicola

WOOD MUSHROOM

The wood mushroom has many similarities to the larger horse mushroom but, as the name suggests, it grows almost exclusively in woodland. Take care, however, not to confuse it with either the yellow stainer, *Agaricus xanthodermus*, or some of the deadly *Amanitas*. Check identifying features carefully. It does not grow out of a volval bag, so there will be no sign of one, and if you turn the mushroom over or cut it you will quite clearly see the identification features. If in any doubt, leave it alone.

IDENTIFICATION

The cap is between 5–10 cm (2–4 in) across, domed at first before opening out to be almost flat. It is a creamy yellow which darkens with age. The stem is 5–8 cm (2–3 in), quite thin and with a clearly marked ring. The gills are mid-pink before turning dark brown. The flesh is white and has a distinct aniseed smell. The spore print is dark brown.

HABITAT AND SEASON

The wood mushroom is quite common in coniferous and deciduous woods. Its season is the autumn.

STORAGE

These mushrooms do not store well, so use and enjoy them as soon as possible after you have picked them.

PREPARATION AND
COOKING HINTS

The young specimens are particularly tasty. Try coating the caps of young mushrooms in seasoned flour, dipping them in a batter made with beer or lager and then deep frying them: delicious.

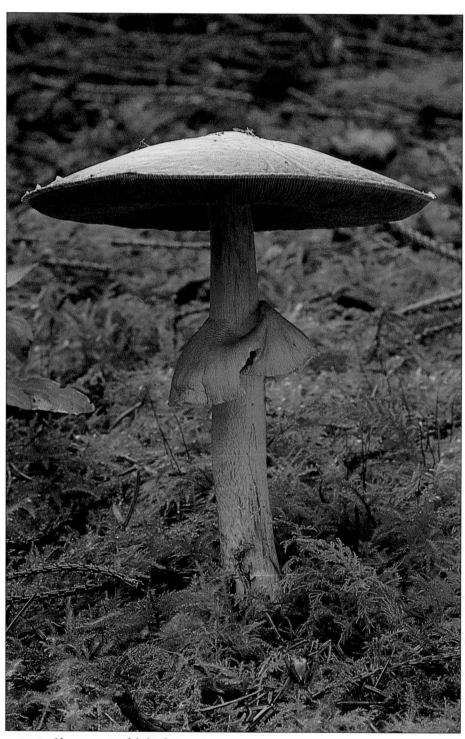

ABOVE *Always a graceful slender mushroom, the wood mushroom grows exclusively inside woodlands.*

Aleuria aurantia
ORANGE PEEL FUNGUS

This wonderfully bright fungus has a nice taste and texture. It is a useful addition to all wild mushroom dishes.

IDENTIFICATION
The cap is small, just under 0.5–5 cm (¼–2 in) across; it is cup-shaped and becomes quite wavy at the edges. The inner surface is bright orange in colour. The underside is much lighter and almost velvety to the touch.

HABITAT AND SEASON
The orange peel fungus grows in fairly large clumps on almost bare earth in light grassland, along roads and in lawns. It is quite common and the season is from autumn through to early winter.

STORAGE
Drying is the best method of storage.

PREPARATION AND COOKING HINTS
Apart from cleaning it carefully, the orange peel fungus needs very little doing to it. It is fairly tough, so can be lightly rinsed in water, then sliced thinly and added to your wild mushroom dishes, to which it will add both flavour and colour.

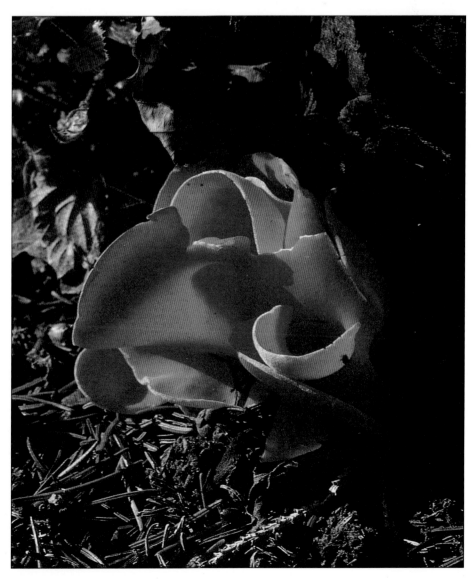

ABOVE RIGHT *Often growing in large clusters, the orange peel fungus prefers disturbed soils along paths and trackways.*

RIGHT *The inner surface (the hymenium) contains the spore-producing cells which are called asci.*

Armillaria mellea

HONEY FUNGUS OR BOOT-LACE FUNGUS

The honey fungus (*Armillaria mellea* and closely related species) is the dreaded enemy of the gardener. This mushroom grows from black cords known as rhizomorphs which can travel enormous distances. They kill the host tree and infect large areas of woodlands. It is, without doubt, the most dangerous of all the tree parasites, causing intensive rot and a very untimely death. If you find honey fungus growing in your garden take specialist advice fast. However, honey fungus is extremely good to eat and grows in very large quantities during the autumn.

IDENTIFICATION

The cap can range from 2–20 cm (¾–7¾ in) across and is also variable in shape and colour. It starts by being convex, then flattens and is centrally depressed. The colour varies from almost honey to dark brown. The stem is 5–15 cm (2–6 in) and can vary quite considerably in width, sometimes being quite tuberous and at

tiny scales at
cap centre

yellow-white,
cottony ring

stem bases fused
together

others very slender. The ring is always clearly visible. The gills vary from off-white to dark brown. The flesh is white with a smell that is quite strong and sweet. The spore print is off-white. It is now thought that there are five or six different forms of honey fungus in Europe. They usually grow in large clumps, either on dead tree trunks, tree stumps or living trees.

HABITAT AND SEASON

Honey fungus is fairly widespread in deciduous and coniferous woods, in-

ABOVE *The scales of the cap vary considerably, ranging from almost smooth as seen here to quite coarse.*

BELOW *When old, the gills can be quite brownish but the spores are pale cream.*

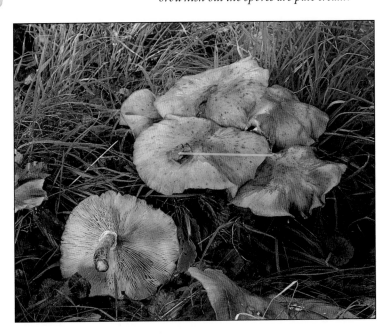

fecting living trees as well as dead trunks and stumps. The season is from early summer to early winter and they can appear several times at the same place during a season.

STORAGE

Drying tends to toughen this mushroom, so it is best to make up dishes first and then freeze them.

PREPARATION AND COOKING HINTS

Only the caps are edible – the stalks are very tough. Boil the caps for two or three minutes in lightly salted water, which must then be discarded as the mushroom may contain a mild toxin. Then cook as you wish. After the initial cooking the caps are particularly good sautéed lightly with onion, garlic and basil, thickened with a little cream and served with pasta.

Auricularia auricula-judae (syn. *Hirneola auricula-judae*)
Jew's Ear or Tree Ear

A common fungus with a very long growing season. It has some looka-likes, so take care with identification.

IDENTIFICATION
The fruit body is 2–7 cm (¾–2¾ in) across with a jelly-like texture and an ear-shaped appearance. In dry weather it becomes hard. It is tan-brown with small greyish hairs on the inner surface.

HABITAT AND SEASON
Grows on a wide variety of trees and is particularly common on elder trees: it gets its name from Judas Iscariot who was said to have been hanged on an elder tree. It has an extremely long growing season and therefore can be collected throughout the year.

STORAGE
Best dried. In fact if they are picked during dry weather when they are hard, they can be stored straight away. Before using, reconstitute by putting in lukewarm water.

PREPARATION AND COOKING HINTS
Wash thoroughly with several changes of water. As they have quite a gelatinous texture it is important to cook them well. A very nice way to serve them is to make a sauce with onions, garlic, basil and finely sliced Jew's ears, thickening it with a little cream, and using it to fill small vol-au-vent cases or to spread on croûtons.

velvety outer surface

inner surface appears smooth and rubbery

LEFT *If in doubt of your identification of this species, try stretching it between your fingers, it should be elastic and rubbery rather than brittle.*

BELOW *The colour can vary greatly. These specimens are very young and fresh and so are quite pale: they may be quite purple-brown with age.*

Boletus badius
BAY BOLETUS

Bay boletus does not become infested with maggots as much as some of the other boletus, but it is still best to pick only clean specimens. The flavour is excellent.

ABOVE *Bay boletus found under conifers (left) are usually darker, smoother and*

more maroon-bay in colour than those found in deciduous woods(right).

IDENTIFICATION
The cap is 4–18 cm (1½–7 in) across, it is usually pale to mid-brown, although lighter specimens may be found. It has a polished appearance, and feels tacky when wet. The stem is 4.5–12.5 cm (1¾–5 in) and similar in colour to the cap. The pores are light yellow, but stain blue if pressed or cut, which is one of the principal identification features of the bay boletus. The white flesh has a faint mushroomy smell, and also stains blue when cut, but the stain soon fades. The spore print is light brown.

HABITAT AND SEASON
In all types of mixed woodland. The season is early summer to late autumn.

STORAGE
A very versatile mushroom. Small specimens may be stored in jars of extra virgin oil, or in wine or cider vinegar. Larger specimens, however, are best sliced and dried after the

pores have been removed, because these will be quite wet and will not dry satisfactorily. These pores can be used in a mushroom ketchup or sauce if you are making one at the time.

PREPARATION AND COOKING HINTS
Bay boletus are best picked when they are dry. Wipe the caps of any wet specimens and let them dry before dealing with them. Thinly sliced, they are delicious eaten raw. However, fresh or dried, the bay boletus is very versatile and can be used in many soups, stews and wild mushroom dishes.

blue-grey stains when bruised

flesh may stain pale blue

no network on stem

Boletus chrysenteron
RED-CRACKED BOLETUS

Although the flavour of this boletus is not as good as that of the bay boletus or the cep, young specimens are good in mixed mushroom dishes.

IDENTIFICATION

The cap is 4–10 cm (1½–4 in) across, snuff brown in colour, but cracks in the surface of the cap often reveal a slightly reddish hue below. However, the red markings on the stem are the real giveaway of this boletus. The stem is 4–8 cm (1½–3 in) with a distinct reddish tinge for most of its length. The pores are yellow and much more open than those of the bay boletus; they stain a light greenish colour. The flesh is cream to yellow and does not bruise on cutting. The spore print is light brown. The overall texture of this mushroom is much less dense than either the bay boletus or the cep.

HABITAT AND SEASON

Found in association with all broadleaved trees. The season is throughout the autumn.

STORAGE

Dry this mushroom before adding it to your other dried mushrooms.

PREPARATION AND COOKING HINTS

Only pick young specimens, wipe or brush the cap to remove any loose particles of earth and slice thinly before cooking. However, because it can be a little mushy, it is best used in soups, stews and mixed dishes with other mushrooms and not on its own.

TOP *As the cap ages, particularly in colder weather, the entire surface may take on a reddish flush.*

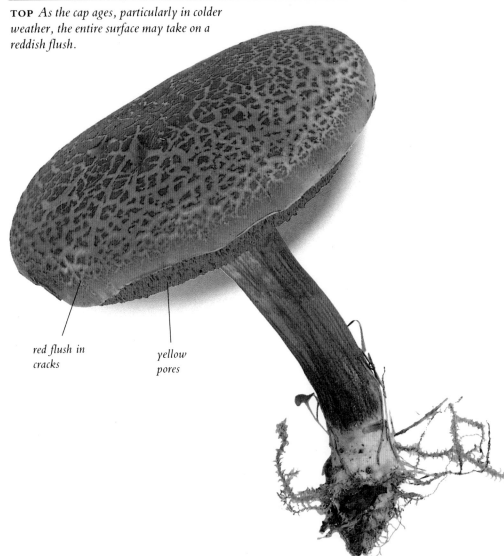

red flush in cracks

yellow pores

41

Boletus edulis
CEP OR PENNY BUN

Mushroom hunters regard this mushroom as a great prize; it has a wonderful nutty flavour and is extremely versatile. It can also grow very big and weigh as much as 1 kg (2 lb 2 oz). It grows over a number of days and flies enter at the base of the stem and the maggots work their way up to the cap and tubes so it is important to pick only those in prime condition. When collecting large specimens cut the cap in half to make sure there is no maggot infestation before putting it in your basket.

IDENTIFICATION
The cap ranges from 6–30 cm (2½–11¾ in) across. Its light brown colour looks rather like freshly baked bread, hence the name 'Penny Bun'. The colour darkens as the cap opens, and it is at this stage that you should examine specimens for maggot infestation. In wet weather the cap can have a slightly sticky appearance, but in dry weather it has a nice velvety sheen. The stem varies from 3–23 cm (1¼–9 in). It is very bulbous and has a fine network, with markings that

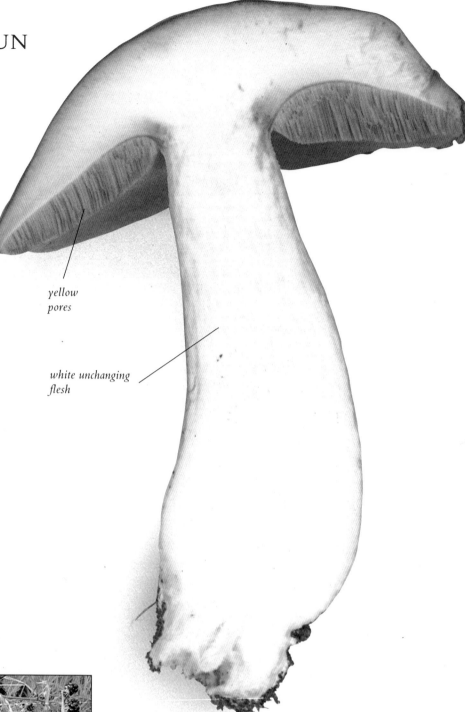

yellow pores

white unchanging flesh

LEFT *Ceps are a great culinary delicacy and they are considered at their best for eating when they are small and tight.*

are more pronounced towards the cap. The pores are white at first, turning light yellow with age. The flesh is quite white and does not change as the mushroom ages. The spore print is light brown.

HABITAT AND SEASON
Coniferous, broad-leaved and mixed woodland; also beside grass pathways. It can also be found in association with heather, along with dwarf willows. The season is summer to late autumn and it is quite common.

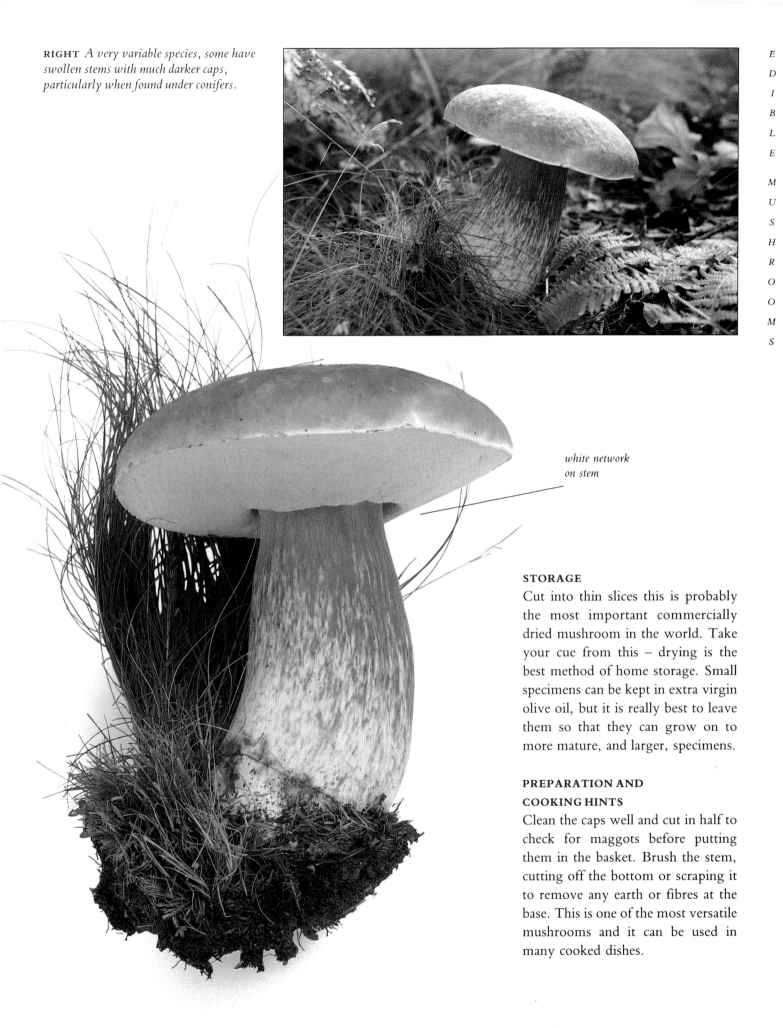

RIGHT *A very variable species, some have swollen stems with much darker caps, particularly when found under conifers.*

white network
on stem

STORAGE

Cut into thin slices this is probably the most important commercially dried mushroom in the world. Take your cue from this – drying is the best method of home storage. Small specimens can be kept in extra virgin olive oil, but it is really best to leave them so that they can grow on to more mature, and larger, specimens.

PREPARATION AND
COOKING HINTS

Clean the caps well and cut in half to check for maggots before putting them in the basket. Brush the stem, cutting off the bottom or scraping it to remove any earth or fibres at the base. This is one of the most versatile mushrooms and it can be used in many cooked dishes.

43

Calocybe gambosa
St George's Mushroom

As its name suggests, St George's mushroom tends to appear around 23 April, St George's Day. It has a great variety of uses and is particularly welcome because it appears early in the year, at much the same time as the common morel. It frequently grows in rings which can be very large, although broken in places. The largest rings may be several hundred years old.

IDENTIFICATION

The cap is 5–15 cm (2–6 in) across with a slightly inrolled margin. Well rounded when young, large old specimens develop an irregular, wavy cap. It is white to cream in colour. The stem is 2–4 cm (¾–1½ in) and white. The gills are narrow and crowded. The flesh is white and soft. It has a mealy smell which is pleasant and strong. The spore print is white.

HABITAT AND SEASON

Tends to grow in rings in grassy locations and around wood edges with underlying chalk. The season is from the beginning of April and into May. For good growth St. George's mushroom relies on warmth and moisture so if the spring is cold it will not appear until the weather becomes warmer. Keep checking areas where you have seen it before.

flesh very thick,
firm and white

gills very crowded
and shallow

stem tough and fibrous

RIGHT *The caps vary from white to a creamy yellow colour.*

BOTTOM *In these mature specimens note how the caps are irregular and wavy.*

STORAGE

St George's mushroom dries extremely well. It can also be stored in virgin olive oil or in vinegar.

PREPARATION AND COOKING HINTS

Brush the caps well because they can be quite gritty and dirty and there may be chalk particles on the underneath. When picking this mushroom always cut the stem to avoid damaging the mycelial rings. It goes particularly well with chicken and fish. Try St. George's chicken, an ordinary chicken casserole given extra zest by the addition of some of these tasty mushrooms.

Cantharellus cibarius
CHANTERELLE

The excitement of finding this mushroom is, for many, the highlight of the mushroom season – not only does it look beautiful, it tastes wonderful. Most collectors are secretive about their chanterelle patches because these mushrooms grow year after year, often in abundant quantities. It is, however, important to ensure you have found the true chanterelle and not simply the false chanterelle, *Hygrophoropsis aurantiaca*.

IDENTIFICATION

The cap is 2–12 cm (¾–4¾ in) across. Flat at first with a broken margin, it later becomes quite fluted with a central depression. The colour can range from very pale to deep yellow, fading a little with age. Occasionally specimens are almost orange. The stem is 3–8 cm (1¼–3 in), very solid and tapered towards the base. The yellow gills are blunt, narrow,

cap depressed
when older

blunt forking
'gills' or ridges

thick pale-yellow
flesh

irregular and run down. the stem. The yellowish flesh has a lovely faint fragrance of apricots – another important identification feature. The spore print is pale cream colour.

HABITAT AND SEASON
In all kinds of woodland which have open mossy clearings. The season is early summer to late autumn.

STORAGE
All forms of storage can be recommended for the chanterelle. It is a particularly interesting one to store in spiced alcohol because of its very fragrant flavour, but it is equally good stored in extra virgin olive oil or vinegar, or else dried.

PREPARATION AND
COOKING HINTS
It is important to clean chanterelles well when you pick them. Brush the caps, and wipe them with a damp cloth if necessary. Cut the stem to avoid any earth getting into your basket. The chanterelle has a good shelf-life: specimens can be kept fresh

for some time either in a refrigerator or in a cool, airy place. They taste exquisite and are wonderfully versatile, whether on their own, in mixed mushroom dishes or with meat or fish dishes. They also give a wonderful colour to sauces and the overall appearance of a dish. Try mixing all different types of *Cantharellus*: this will combine the different flavours and textures and make a wonderfully colourful dish of wild mushrooms.

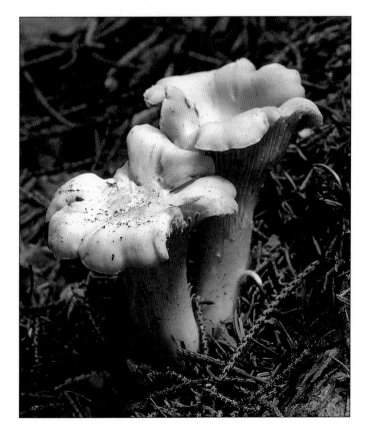

LEFT *Observe how the 'gills' of this species are very shallow, blunt and frequently forked, more like deep wrinkles or veins than true gills.*

Cantharellus infundibuliformis
WINTER CHANTERELLE

The winter chanterelle is so called because it usually appears much later than the ordinary chanterelle. It is quite an achievement to find these tiny little gems hidden under falling autumn leaves. But once you get your eye in you will find troops of them growing where before you had hardly seen anything. They tend to grow in the same place each year, so note where you find them.

IDENTIFICATION
The cap is 2–5 cm (¾–2 in) across, convex at first, soon becoming funnel-shaped with a fluted edge. It is dark brown on top, very much the same colour as the leaf litter under which it grows. The stem is 5–8 cm (2–3 in), yellow and hollow. The gills are narrow and quite irregular,

greyish-lilac forked gills or wrinkles

hollow stem

yellowish at first they are greyish lilac in older specimens. The flesh is yellowish and smells faintly sweet. The spore print is yellow.

HABITAT AND SEASON

Grows in large numbers in both deciduous and coniferous woods, preferring acid soil. The season is from late summer to late autumn.

STORAGE

Winter chanterelles dry extremely well, but can also be stored in extra virgin olive oil or wine vinegar.

PREPARATION AND COOKING HINTS

As these usually grow through leaf litter they are quite clean, so all they are likely to need is a dusting with your brush. And if you cut the stalks rather than pulling them up, you will avoid earth and other debris. They are very versatile in cooking, with an extremely nice, sweet flavour that goes especially well with fish.

brown cap surface

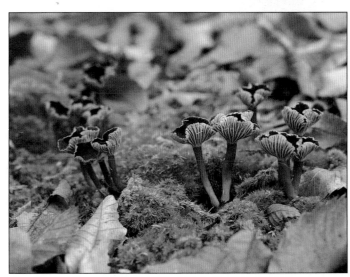

ABOVE *A good tip for finding these mushrooms is to follow woodland streams and search on the mossy banks as this is one of their favourite habitats.*

ABOVE *When growing in fallen leaves winter chanterelles are very difficult to spot.*

Clitocybe odora
ANISEED TOADSTOOL

The aniseed toadstool is most useful as a condiment. Take care when you identify it, because the verdigris agaric, *Stropharia aeruginosa*, looks rather similar, although it has a blunt knob at centre when open, and is always sticky and darkish-green in colour. As the name suggests, the aniseed toadstool has a very pungent aniseed smell.

IDENTIFICATION
The cap is 3–7 cm (1¼–2¾ in) across; button-shaped at first, it soon flattens and sometimes becomes wavy. The colour is a blue-green which darkens

cap surface is dry, not sticky

gills are pale greenish-white

no ring on stem

RIGHT AND BELOW *This lookalike, Stropharia aeruginosa, has a sticky cap and a ring on the stem. It has no odour. The gills turn purple-brown when mature.*

BOTTOM *The colour may fade rapidly from that shown to almost white. These specimens are best avoided in case of confusion with the suspect Clitocybe fragrans, which is white and also smells of aniseed.*

with age. The stem is 3–6 cm (1¼–2½ in) and lightly striated. The gills, which are not very marked, are close and run down the stem. The flesh is pale and the smell is strongly of aniseed. The spore print is white.

HABITAT AND SEASON
In leaf litter along the edges of coniferous and deciduous woods. In the latter they are likely to be in association with beech or sweet chestnut.

The season is from late summer to late autumn and they are relatively common.

STORAGE
Best dried and stored separately because of the intensity of its flavour.

PREPARATION AND COOKING HINTS
Best used as a flavouring: finely chop fresh specimens or powder dried ones.

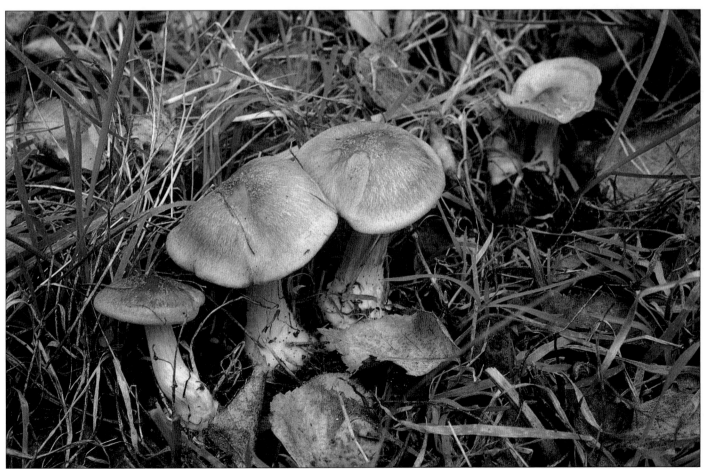

Coprinus comatus

SHAGGY INK CAP OR LAWYER'S WIG

One of the most common mush-rooms, they often come up in dense clusters on newly turned earth in meadows and gardens throughout the summer. Only the young speci-mens are edible and once picked they must be used quickly, otherwise they soon decay into a nasty inky mass. This is an easy mushroom to identify as it is very distinct, although care must be taken that the early stages of this and the magpie fungus, *Coprinus picaceus*, are not mistaken. However, the magpie fungus has something like a veil which the shaggy ink cap does not.

IDENTIFICATION
The cap is 5–12 cm (2–4¾ in) across; egg-shaped at first, it opens to a bell. White with a cream-coloured centre; it has large shaggy scales. The stem is 10–37 cm (4–14½ in) and white. The gills are white to start with, slowly changing to black from the edge in-wards before becoming a mass of ink which, incidentally, makes good drawing ink. The flesh is white with a slight sweet smell. The spore print is brown-black.

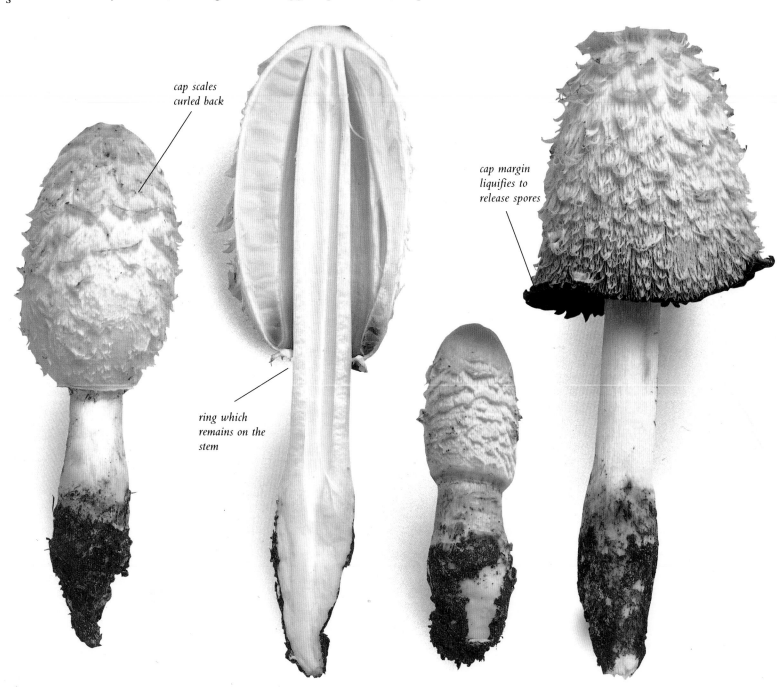

cap scales curled back

ring which remains on the stem

cap margin liquifies to release spores

BELOW *The very distinct narrow ring is not easily seen here, but as the cap expands it will be left behind on the stem.*

HABITAT AND SEASON

Widespread on grassy banks beside roads, on rubbish heaps, lawns and recently disturbed soil near building sites. The season is midsummer to late autumn. They are very common.

STORAGE

Best used fresh or dried in an electric drier. Do not attempt to air-dry them as they will turn into an inky mass.

PREPARATION AND COOKING HINTS

Although shaggy ink caps can be used dried; they are really best fresh, either on their own, or with the parasol mushroom, *Lepiota procera*, to make a wonderful soup. Use the two mushrooms, some onions and a little potato to thicken, sweated together and then liquidized. Simple and quite delicious.

ABOVE *This is the best stage to collect shaggy ink caps for cooking.*

LEFT *Magpie fungus,* Coprinus picaceus *can be confused with the shaggy ink cap in its early stages.*

Craterellus cornucopioides

HORN OF PLENTY OR TROMPETTE DES MORTS

Another wonderful mushroom of the *Cantharellus* family. Like the chanterelle and winter chanterelle, the horn of plenty appears in large groups in the same place year after year. These, however, are quite often covered by leaf litter and are difficult to spot because of their colour. Although the initial appearance is not inviting, the taste is excellent.

IDENTIFICATION

The cap is 2–9 cm (¾–3½ in) across; it is shaped like a tube or a trumpet and has an open flared mouth and is hollow. It becomes irregular with age and is thin and tough. In colour it ranges from mid-brown to black, though it fades with age. The gills are barely perceptible. The flesh is grey to black. The spore print is white.

HABITAT AND SEASON

Grows in large clusters among the leaf litter of deciduous woods. The season is from late summer to quite late autumn.

STORAGE

All forms of storage are appropriate for the horn of plenty, but it is probably best dried.

trumpet-like
depression

smooth to
slightly wrinkled
surface

PREPARATION AND COOKING HINTS

Remember that these mushrooms are hollow. You will always need to brush them and, with larger specimens, it is best to slice them in half and remove any debris that has gone down the funnel-cap. The horn of plenty is very versatile in cooking, but goes particularly well with fish, its dark colour making a striking contrast with white fish.

completely hollow

BELOW *Like the winter chanterelle, this species is found in damp mossy banks alongside streams and in deep leaf litter.*

Fistulina hepatica
BEEFSTEAK FUNGUS

An important bracket fungus from a collector's point of view, not only is it interesting in colour and texture, it has a good flavour. Because the beefsteak fungus often grows fairly high up trees, you may well need to add a ladder to your collecting equipment.

IDENTIFICATION
The bracket can vary from 8–30 cm (3–11¾ in) across and is quite thick. It is usually in a single piece, although several may grow one above the other. Cut through, the beefsteak fungus really does look rather like a piece of meat. The colour of the bracket is an orange-red darkening with age, the pores are much lighter. The flesh is thick, succulent and mottled dark red; it has quite a pleasant smell. The spore print is brown.

HABITAT AND SEASON
Grows on chestnut or oak trees, usually, but not always, on the lower part of the trunk. Season is late summer to autumn, although it may appear earlier. Although this fungus causes rot inside a tree it does not kill it, but it makes the wood of infected trees much darker. Oak darkened in this way is in demand in the furniture

cut flesh 'bleeds' red juice

pores pull apart very easily

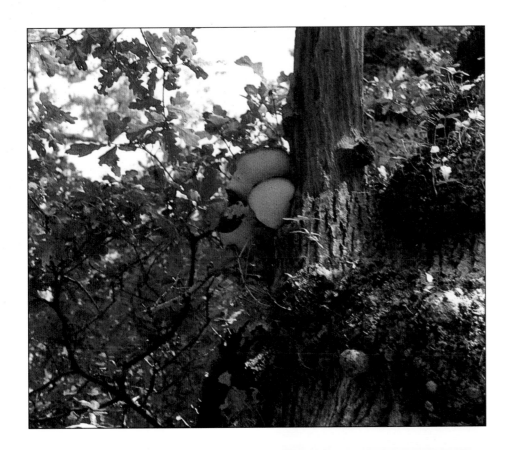

LEFT *Beefsteak fungi often grow very high up in trees. Another good clue to identifying this species is that the individual tubes separate from each other very easily, unlike all other bracket fungi.*

BELOW *The upper surface can be very moist and spongy when fresh.*

industry. Near Holt, in north Norfolk, England, there is a 980-year-old oak tree with beefsteak fungus growing up to a height of 12 m (40 ft) from the base, a little bit difficult from a picker's point of view, but nevertheless a wonderful sight.

STORAGE

Like other bracket fungi this will toughen if dried, so it is best to make dishes and then freeze them.

PREPARATION AND
COOKING HINTS

Cut off any parts of the tree still attached to the fungus. Separate the various layers and wipe them with a damp cloth. The beefsteak fungus has a slightly metallic taste, so it is best to slice it into strips and soak these in milk for about two hours to remove the slight acidity and acrid flavour. Then it can be grilled as a piece of steak with a little onion, basil and garlic. Try it, too, on a charcoal grill or barbecue. It is also excellent added to soups and stews for extra flavour and colour.

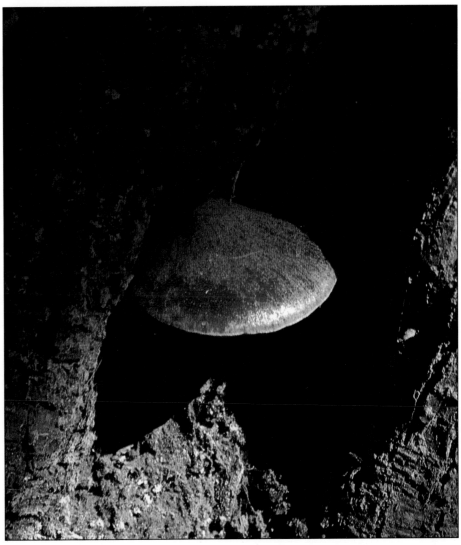

Flammulina velutipes
VELVET SHANK

As the name implies, the velvet shank has a dark velvety stem. It normally grows during the winter months and can survive the frosts, indeed it may need a frost before starting to grow. It can be frozen solid, but still survive.

IDENTIFICATION

The cap is 3–10 cm (1¼–4 in) across and fairly flat. It is light orange in colour, paler at the edges and darker towards the centre. It is also quite smooth and shiny with a sticky surface. The stem is 1–3 cm (½–1¼ in), very tough and is, as the name suggests, velvety and dark in colour, particularly at the base. The flesh, which is yellow on the cap changing to dark brown on the stem, has little smell. The gills are pale yellow. The spore print is white.

HABITAT AND SEASON

The velvet shank often grows in very large clusters on dead or decaying wood, particularly in association with elm and oak, and also gorse roots. The season is long because they grow all through the winter months and so are useful when only a limited number of mushrooms is available.

STORAGE

The best method of storage is to dry and powder them.

PREPARATION AND COOKING HINTS

As they have a fairly tough texture they really are best dried. If using them fresh, cut off most of the stem, and slice the caps finely. Use to give a good flavour to soups and stews, but remember to cook them well.

dense clusters of stems

black, velvety stem base

no ring on stem

LEFT *Difficult to confuse with anything else because of the unusual season of growth but note the absence of a ring on the stem. Poisonous lookalikes will have a ring or a veil.*

Grifola frondosa (syn. Polyporus frondosus)
HEN OF THE WOODS

This is an unusual fungus which, like the cauliflower fungus, grows at the base of tree trunks and can be extremely large. Its many caps are joined together and a large specimen can provide a feast for many people. Good to eat and quite rare, so note where you find it as it will certainly grow there again.

IDENTIFICATION

The fruit body is 10–15 cm (4–6 in) across, and consists of a central section with many branch stems ending in individual caps. Each cap is 3–7 cm (1¼–2¾ in) across and has quite a wrinkled edge. The whole fruit body is greyish in colour turning brown with age. The stems are pale grey. The hen of the woods has tubes rather than gills. These are 2–3 mm (¹⁄₁₀ in) long and run down the stem. The flesh, which is white, has a slightly musty smell.

HABITAT AND SEASON

Grows at the base of the trunks of oaks or other deciduous trees. Occasionally it grows on tree stumps. The season of the hen of the woods is autumn to early winter.

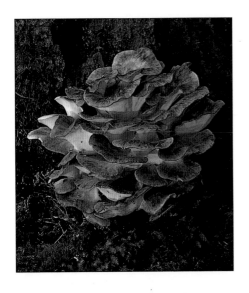

STORAGE

The best method of storage is drying. Otherwise freeze dishes in which you have used this mushroom.

PREPARATION AND COOKING HINTS

It is important to clean the hen of the woods thoroughly as it has many nooks and crevices which harbour dirt. Due to its very tough texture it can be rinsed in cold water prior to cooking. It tastes good and goes well in a wide variety of wild mushroom dishes, but, because of its tough texture, make sure it is well cooked. Dried and then powdered, it can be added to soups and stews.

59

Hydnum repandum
HEDGEHOG FUNGUS

spines on underside of cap

very thick tough stems

thick, peppery tasting flesh

This little gem is often quite difficult to find on the woodland floor. Perseverance pays as it has great culinary value and is much sought after by collectors.

IDENTIFICATION
The cream-coloured caps are usually single and 2–15 cm (¾–6 in) across, flattening with a slight central depression and rolled rim. The stem is 3.5–7.5 cm (1¼–3 in) and quite bulbous. It is quite downy and is white, bruising slightly yellow when cut. In place of pores or veins, this mushroom has little spines, hence the name hedgehog fungus. The flesh is white with a very pleasant smell. The spore print is cream-coloured.

HABITAT AND SEASON
Grows in large numbers and under deciduous or coniferous trees, usually in quite damp situations such as along drainage ditches or where there are mossy patches. The season is late summer to late autumn.

STORAGE
These are best sliced and dried for winter use, although they can be kept in oil or vinegar.

PREPARATION AND COOKING HINTS
After cleaning, the smaller specimens can be cooked whole or else sliced. With larger specimens it is probably best to remove the spines, as although quite edible they look like small hairs and could spoil the appearance of the finished dish. This is a very versatile mushroom, going very well with both meat and fish dishes, but it is worth trying some on their own for their excellent flavour.

LEFT *The cap colour can vary from pinkish-buff to this rare white form.*

Hypholoma sublateritium
BRICK CAP

These small mushrooms, which appear in clusters in the autumn, are good to eat. However, it is quite easy to confuse them with the sulphur tuft, *Hypholoma fasciculare*, which is poisonous, so it is important to take care over identifying them.

IDENTIFICATION
The cap is 4–10 cm (1½–4 in) across and quite convex, although it can flatten in mature specimens. As the name suggests, the cap is brick red, darkest in the centre and often paler towards the margins. The stem is 5–18 cm (2–7 in) long and whitish, but can stain darker when cut. It has a partial veil. The gills are purplish-grey. The flesh is pale yellow and

BELOW *Note the veil remnants on the cap margin and the robust, fleshy caps and stems. These specimens are unusually wet and sticky.*

BOTTOM *Note how the gills flush purple as the spores mature. They are never greenish-yellow like the sulphur tuft.*

slightly darker towards the stem. It has a definite smell of mushrooms. The spore print is purple-brown.

HABITAT AND SEASON
The brick cap grows in clusters on the stumps of old deciduous trees, from late autumn to early winter.

STORAGE
Only keep the caps, which are best dried whole for storage.

PREPARATION AND COOKING HINTS
Only collect the young specimens when they are at their very best. Cooked lightly these give a good flavour to any dish.

Laccaria amethystea
AMETHYST DECEIVER

The amethyst deceiver grows in large troops. It is colourful, edible and tasty, and so makes excellent additions to your cooking.

IDENTIFICATION
The cap is 1–5 cm (½–2 in) across. It is convex but flattens with age and develops a slight depression in the centre. Deep purplish-lilac in colour, it dries to an almost buff colour. The stem is 4–10 cm (1½–4 in), hollow and has slightly white fibres below the cap. The gills are a similar colour to the cap. The flesh is thin and tinged lilac. The smell is not distinctive. The spore print is white.

HABITAT AND SEASON
Grows in coniferous and deciduous woods, often with beech and chestnut. The season is late summer to early winter. It is very common.

STORAGE
Dries very well. It can also be stored in spiced alcohol to give a most unusual sauce to serve over ice-cream and desserts.

PREPARATION AND COOKING HINTS
As these grow quite densely and have wide open gills, they can be dirty, so it is important to clean them well before using. If you store them in spiced alcohol, blanch them first. It is important that if stored in alcohol these are kept in a refrigerator to prevent fermentation. They are also excellent fresh.

cap becomes much paler when dry

LEFT *When picked, amethyst deceivers are bright in colour but this will fade.*

Laccaria laccata
DECEIVER

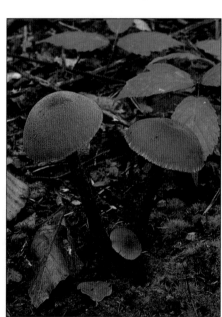

Like the amethyst deceiver, the deceiver grows in large troops.

IDENTIFICATION

The deceiver has a cap that can be slightly larger than the amethyst deceiver, but is also convex and flattening. It can open to look like a chanterelle. The colour is tawny to pale red and it dries to a paler colour. The stem is 5–10 cm (2–4 in), a similar colour to the cap, but often is twisted. The gills are well spread. The flesh is a pale reddish-brown and the smell is not distinctive. The spore print is white.

HABITAT AND SEASON

Grows in coniferous and deciduous woods. The season is late summer to early winter. They are very common.

STORAGE

The best method of storage is drying.

PREPARATION AND COOKING HINTS

Like the amethyst deceiver, it is important to clean it well before putting it in your basket. Follow the instructions on the opposite page for spicing in alcohol.

RIGHT, ABOVE AND BELOW *The deceiver is incredibly variable and it may take you many seasons to recognize the many variations.*

Lactarius deliciosus
SAFFRON MILK-CAP

A lovely, colourful mushroom to find. It grows very close to the ground and often on quite sandy soil, which can make cleaning difficult. It also has a hollow stem which can lead to problems with infestation. To avoid this problem just pick young fresh specimens, but make sure that they are mature enough for a positive identification, otherwise they can be confused with the woolly milk-cap, *Lactarius torminosus*, or *Lactarius pubescens*, both of which are poisonous.

IDENTIFICATION

The cap is 3–12 cm (1¼–4¾ in) across, convex with a depressed centre. It has concentric rings and, as the name suggests, is saffron in colour.

ABOVE *As you can see, the cap becomes pale, almost silvery-white or dull greenish with age. Pick the fresher orange caps.*

cap with
concentric rings

stains green
when bruised

bleeds orange
milk when cut

On cutting you will notice that it bleeds a saffron colour. It also has a clean, inrolled edge. This is an important means of identification, because neither the woolly milk-cap nor *Lactarius pubescens* have clean edges to the cap. The hollow stem is 3–6 cm (1¼–2½ in) pale, blotched with orange, and when bruised or broken, turns greenish. The closely spaced gills are saffron in colour. The flesh is pale. The saffron milk-cap is brighter in colour than either of its lookalikes, which is a useful aid to identification.

HABITAT AND SEASON

Always grows under pine or spruce trees, and can also be found beside paths on sandy heathland. The season is early summer to quite late autumn.

STORAGE

This stores extremely well, whether dried or in oil or vinegar.

PREPARATION AND
COOKING HINTS

The sand and pine needles of this mushroom's habitat make cleaning important. Indeed, it may be necessary to wash your specimens immediately before cooking, but then dry them well before slicing and cooking them. The lovely crunchy texture and good flavour make this a much sought-after mushroom.

RIGHT *The cap margin is shaggy in these young specimens.*

Laetiporus sulphureus
SULPHUR POLYPORE OR CHICKEN OF THE WOODS

One of the more spectacular of all bracket fungi, this can grow in very large quantities and come quite early in the mushroom season. Its versatility makes it important from a culinary point of view, but only pick young specimens.

IDENTIFICATION

The bracket can range from 15–50 cm (6–19¾ in) across. Often the shape of a fan, it has a semi-circular growing habit and quite nice rounded edges. The colour is spectacular; lemon to orange-yellow, although it tends to darken with age. The brackets have an almost velvet-like appearance. It has yellow tubes. The flesh in young specimens is tender and exudes a yellow juice. The smell is quite pungent and a little acrid.

HABITAT AND SEASON

Grows on deciduous trees, particularly oak and sweet chestnut, but may also be found on yew, cherry and willow. The season is usually from late spring to early autumn, but if the winter has been mild it will often appear much earlier, so keep a look out for it.

STORAGE

Drying toughens this mushroom, so it is best used fresh and the finished dish frozen.

PREPARATION AND COOKING HINTS

Avoid the toughest specimens and only use young ones. Cleaning can be difficult but it is best to separate the individual layers, brushing lightly; bearing in mind that the dense texture makes it possible to wash it to remove any infestation or dirt. To remove the slight bitter taste blanch it for two to three minutes in boiling, salted water prior to cooking. The texture and flavour is of chicken, as the name suggests, and it is much prized by chefs. It is wonderful for vegetarian meals, making an excellent chicken of the woods risotto or chicken of the woods curry.

BELOW *The giant polypore,* Meripilus giganteus, *can reach 1½ m (4 ft) across. Its flesh stains black when bruised but it is edible when very young.*

BELOW LEFT AND BELOW *When young, the strange lumpy growths of* Laetiporus sulphureus *can look quite unlike the elegant brackets it will form with age.*

BOTTOM *This bracket lasts quite a while in the field and when old is soft, spongy and paler in colour. Pick the brightly coloured fruit bodies.*

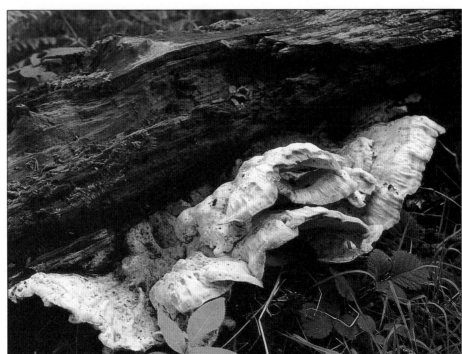

Langermannia gigantea
GIANT PUFF-BALL

The giant puff-ball can be truly spectacular. It is also versatile in the kitchen, but only pick specimens that are fresh and young and sound hollow when you tap the top of the mushroom. It is pointless picking this mushroom once the flesh has become discoloured. Check its age by cutting the specimen right through; the knife should not tear the flesh but pass crisply through it.

IDENTIFICATION

The fruit body can range from 5–80 cm (2–31½ in) across, although specimens of 120 cm (48 in) across have been recorded. When young it has a nice white appearance, although the outer wall may break away to expose the spore mass and become yellow. Avoid at this stage.

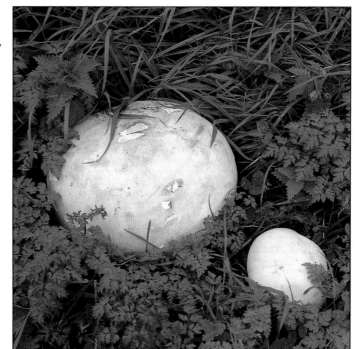

LEFT *Hedgerows and ditch banks are two of the favourite habitats of the giant puff-ball.*

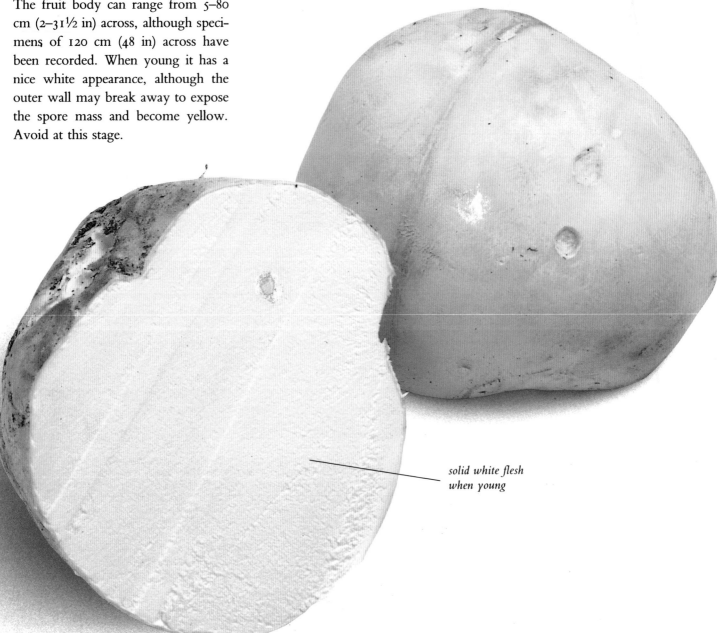

solid white flesh
when young

HABITAT AND SEASON

Grows in gardens, pastures, woodlands and a wide variety of other situations, such as along dyke banks. The season is any time from early summer to late autumn unless the weather is very dry, when it will not grow. There will usually be several in the same area and they grow in the same place year after year.

STORAGE

There is no satisfactory way of storing giant puff-balls, so it is best to make up the dishes and freeze them.

PREPARATION AND COOKING HINTS

Very little needs to be done to this mushroom. Wipe the specimens carefully with a damp cloth and, if you are not going to use them immediately, wrap in cling film and keep in the refrigerator for up to three days. The giant puff-ball goes extremely well in all wild mushroom dishes, soups and stews. It also makes a good breakfast sliced and fried with bacon or else dipped in beaten egg and breadcrumbs and lightly fried in bacon fat.

LEFT AND ABOVE *This shows another large edible species,* Lycoperdon excipuliforme, *which frequently grows in large clusters. It is common in woodlands.*

Leccinum scabrum

BROWN BIRCH BOLETE

Although the brown birch bolete is not as well favoured as the orange birch bolete, it is still quite useful in the kitchen. However, only pick young firm specimens as older ones tend to absorb a good deal of moisture and so have a very soft texture.

IDENTIFICATION

The cap is 5–12 cm (2–4¾ in) across and mid-brown in colour. It is dry, but can be slightly sticky in wet weather. The stem is 7–20 cm (2¾–7¾ in), white with brown to blackish flecked scales. The pores are brown. The flesh is white and the smell quite pleasant. The spore print is brown.

HABITAT AND SEASON

Grows under birch trees. The season is summer to late autumn.

STORAGE

Drying is the best method of storage. Cut it into sections and either air-dry or use an electric dryer.

PREPARATION AND COOKING HINTS

As this mushroom has quite a soft texture, it is best to use it in conjunction with other mushrooms in a mixed mushroom dish or in mushroom soups.

flesh may redden in some forms

slightly sticky smooth cap

RIGHT *The brown birch bolete has recently been subdivided into a number of closely related species, all of which are edible.*

Leccinum versipelle
ORANGE BIRCH BOLETE

A bolete that is particularly good to eat. It can grow to a fairly large size and, as the name implies, is usually in close association with birch trees.

IDENTIFICATION

The cap is 6–25 cm (2½–9¾ in) across. It is a lovely orange colour and has a slightly fluffy appearance at first before becoming smooth or scaly depending on the weather conditions. It is usually dry. The stem can be up to 20 cm (7¾ in). It is white to greyish in colour and covered with brown to blackish scales. The stems of young specimens bruise a bright electric blue in patches. The pores are off-white to grey. The flesh is pale, becoming blackish with age. The smell is quite pleasant. When cut in cross-section this mushroom stains quite black on the inside, but you should not be put off by this as it is good to eat. The spore print is light brown.

HABITAT AND SEASON

Grows in association with birch and scrub. The season is midsummer to quite late autumn.

STORAGE

Because this mushroom can be quite large, it is best to slice it before drying, which is the best way of storing it.

PREPARATION AND
COOKING HINTS

It should only be necessary to wipe the cap with a damp cloth and brush any loose dust particles from the stem. A versatile mushroom, it is much sought after by chefs.

flesh turns reddish-lilac then black when cut

stem scales darken with handling

leaves of birch, the preferred host tree

ABOVE *The caps may expand to a much greater size in proportion to the stem than is shown here and the colour can fade to dull yellow buff.*

ABOVE *The cap may become quite felty and scaly with age, particularly at the centre.*

Lepista nuda (syn. *Tricholoma nudum*)

WOOD BLEWIT

The wood blewit is useful because it appears late in the season. But beware – some people are allergic to it. Make sure you try only a little first and take care if you serve it to guests. It is also most important to remember it must be well cooked and never eaten raw.

IDENTIFICATION

The cap is 6–12 cm (2½–4¾ in) across. Convex at first, it eventually flattens and is sometimes quite convoluted. The cap starts by being quite blue but then turns an almost shiny tan. It dries a little paler. The stem is 5–9 cm (2–3½ in) and often has purple markings. The gills are crowded and very lilac, although they lose their colour with age they never turn brown. It is best to pick younger specimens that still retain the wonderful colour for they have the best flavour. The flesh is bluish and the smell is quite perfumed. The spore print is pale pink.

gills remain violet, never turn brown

smooth cap surface

tough, fibrous stem

HABITAT AND SEASON

Grows in all mixed woodland, hedgerows and gardens and sometimes on open ground. The season is from autumn to early winter. It is quite common and often grows in large quantities.

STORAGE

Because the wood blewit must be cooked before it is eaten, it is best not to dry it. It does, however, keep extremely well if it is blanched and then put in wine vinegar, extra virgin olive oil or spiced alcohol. But, if kept in the alcohol, it must be stored in the refrigerator to stop fermentation. The colour and fragrance of this mushroom mean it can be used in both sweet and savoury dishes.

PREPARATION AND
COOKING HINTS

Quite an easy mushroom to clean, gently wipe the top and cut the stem. It is good in all mushroom dishes, but as it has a very strong flavour it goes particularly well with strongly flavoured vegetables such as onions and leeks. Try a blewit bake by mixing onions, leeks and wood blewits in a béchamel sauce. Do not forget, however, that some people are allergic to it.

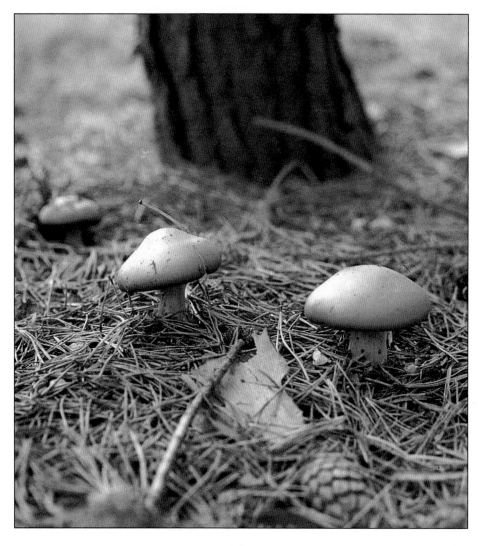

TOP *Note that the caps are smooth and not sticky. The gills remain violet, never turning rusty brown as do those of some lookalike species, such as* Cortinarius.

RIGHT *Although these specimens are under pines, the wood blewit is equally common in deciduous woods and gardens.*

Lepista saeva
FIELD BLEWIT OR BLUE LEG

The field blewit is most commonly found exactly where the name suggests. But, because they are low-growing, they are difficult to spot in long grass. Its other name, blue leg, comes from the brightly coloured stem. It is best picked young, to avoid infestation with maggots. Remember, like the wood blewit, this mushroom must be cooked before it is eaten and some people are allergic to it, so take care.

IDENTIFICATION
The cap is 6–12 cm (2½–4¾ in) across. Quite convex at first then flattening, it can be slightly depressed

these are in perfect condition for picking

when fully opened out. The cap is a rather insignificant buff colour, but it has a nice shine. The stem, which is 3–6 cm (1¼–2½ in) is the most significant thing about the field blewit. It is often rather bulbous and has lilac markings. The gills are crowded and whitish. The flesh is quite thick and chunky and white to flesh-coloured. It has a perfumed smell very similar to that of the wood blewit. The spore print is pale pink.

HABITAT AND SEASON
Often grows in large numbers in rings in pastureland. The season is

autumn through to the first frosts of winter, although it can stand some light frosts.

STORAGE

As this is another mushroom that must be cooked before it is eaten, it is best blanched and stored in wine vinegar or extra virgin olive oil. Store in spiced alcohol if you want to serve it as a dessert.

PREPARATION AND
COOKING HINTS

Very similar to the wood blewit, the field blewit gives a really good flavour to stews if it is chopped up first.

ABOVE *Here, you can see clearly the complete lack of violet colour in the cap, compared to the wood blewit.*

no violet in gills

bluish-lilac stem may fade when old

Macrolepiota procera
PARASOL MUSHROOM

BELOW *Usually found in fields, not in woodlands, where some related species grow.*

BELOW LEFT *Note the coarse brown scales on the cap, the white ring and bands of brown scales on the stem.*

The parasol mushroom can grow quite large and has a long growing season. They reappear in the same place year after year, and may well have several flushes of growth during the season. The name is appropriate for this mushroom does indeed look like a lady's parasol.

IDENTIFICATION
The cap, which is 10–25 cm (4–9¾ in) or more, starts by being very spherical, but soon flattens out though retaining a prominent centre. It is pale buff in colour and covered with symmetrical patterns of dark shaggy scales. The stem is 15–30 cm (6–11¾ in), white and has a large ring, the gills are white. The flesh is thin and white and has a fairly sweet, although not particularly distinctive, smell. The spore print is white. This mushroom is usually maggot-free and is best collected when dry as it soon absorbs moisture, becoming soggy and almost unusable.

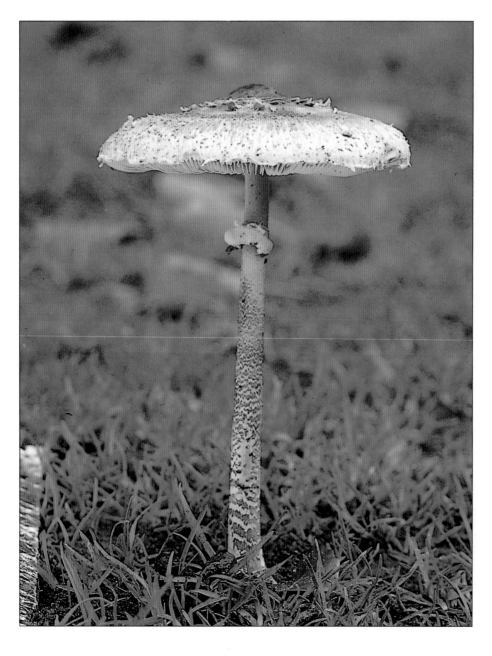

HABITAT AND SEASON
In open woods and pastures, and along roadside hedges. The season is from early summer to late autumn.

STORAGE
This mushroom dries well. Discard the stems, which are tough, cut the cap into segments and dry. It reconstitutes well and makes an excellent addition to soups and stews.

PREPARATION AND COOKING HINTS
This mushroom is usually clean and maggot-free, so very little attention needs to be paid to cleaning. However, dust off any particles on the top, remove the stalk right into the cap and cut into segments. An excellent, if unusual, way of using it is to make up a batter with beer or lager instead of milk, dipping the pieces into the batter and then deep-frying them. Alternatively, you can dust the segments of cap in seasoned flour and shallow- or deep-fry. Cooked like this it makes a crisp starter to a meal or a good addition to a main course.

Macrolepiota rhacodes
SHAGGY PARASOL

The shaggy parasol is smaller than the parasol mushroom. Although it is edible it can cause stomach upsets, a point to remember when serving it to guests.

IDENTIFICATION
The cap is 5–12 cm (2–4¾ in) across; ovate at first, it expands to become almost flat. It gets its name from the cap's shaggy appearance. The markings are not as clear as those of the parasol, but it has quite a fibrous appearance. The stem is 10–15 cm (4–6 in), off-white with a pinky-brown tinge. The gills are white at first, becoming tinged with red as it ages. The white-tinged flesh bruises reddish-brown or pink. When cut it turns red. The smell is aromatic. The spore print is white.

HABITAT AND SEASON
Grows in woods and shrubberies of all kinds, often with conifers as well as under hedges and along roadside verges. The season is early summer to late autumn.

STORAGE
A mushroom that dries extremely well. Discard the stalk, cut the cap into sections and dry. Reconstituted, it is excellent in soups and stews or mixed wild mushroom dishes.

PREPARATION AND COOKING HINTS
Very similar to the parasol. The shaggy parasol has a clean cap which needs very little attention other than a light brushing. If using fresh specimens, discard the stalk and cut the cap into segments, then deep fry or add to mushroom dishes. The smaller caps are good for stuffing.

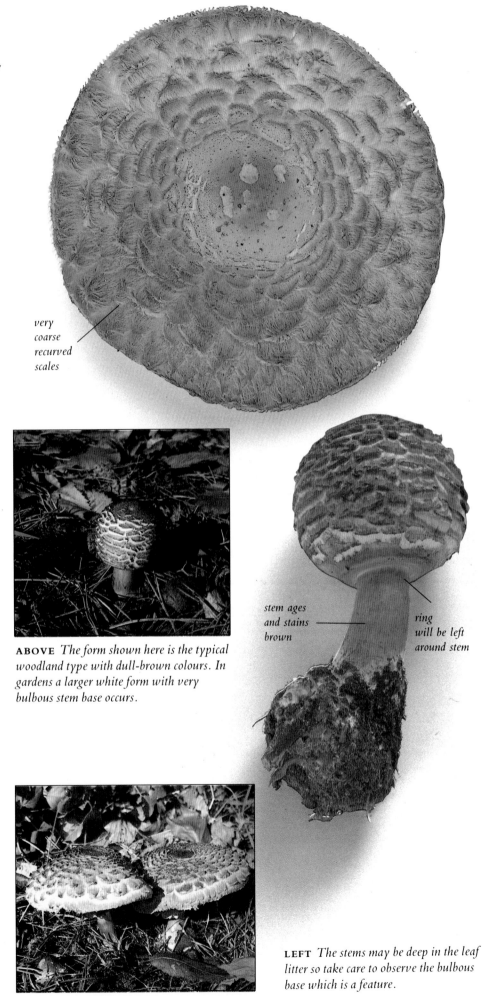

very coarse recurved scales

ABOVE *The form shown here is the typical woodland type with dull-brown colours. In gardens a larger white form with very bulbous stem base occurs.*

stem ages and stains brown

ring will be left around stem

LEFT *The stems may be deep in the leaf litter so take care to observe the bulbous base which is a feature.*

Marasmius oreades
FAIRY RING CHAMPIGNON OR FAIRY RING FUNGUS

One of the first mushrooms to appear in spring, the fairy ring champignon tastes just as good as it looks. But beware, there is a poisonous looka-like, the *Clitocybe rivulosa*, that grows in a very similar way in very similar situations. It is most important to learn to identify these two. There is very little similarity once they are full grown, but it is important not to make any mistakes.

IDENTIFICATION
The cap is 2–5 cm (¾–2 in) across, convex at first, then flattening with quite a marked centre. Tan in colour, it dries to a fairly light buff. The stem is 2–10 cm (¾–4 in) and tough, so it is best when picking to remove the stem entirely. The gills are white to tan and quite distant. The flesh is thick. The spore print is white.

HABITAT AND SEASON
It forms rings in the shorter grass of old pastures or lawns. The season is from the spring to late autumn. It is very common. It is essential to be able to distinguish between this mushroom and *Clitocybe rivulosa*. The latter also grows in rings often very close, within a metre, to those of the fairy ring champignon. The colour and gills are quite different and *Clitocybe rivulosa* does not appear so early in the year, but it is important that you can identify them.

caps darker
when young

tough
fibrous stems

gills do not
run down the stem

widely spaced
thick gills,
pale brown in colour

LEFT This classic fairy ring is a few metres across, but they may reach over a hundred metres!

STORAGE

These mushrooms are wonderful eaten fresh, but also dry very well. They can also be stored in spiced Cinzano, extra virgin olive oil or wine or cider vinegar after blanching.

PREPARATION AND
COOKING HINTS

As long as you pick these mushrooms clean and cut off the stems when picking them from grass, the only problem you are likely to have is removing a few blades of grass. Occasionally a light dusting with a brush may be necessary, but washing definitely spoils the flavour. From a culinary point of view this is a versatile mushroom, going extremely well with meat and fish dishes as well as mixed mushroom dishes.

BELOW Note how the grass is shorter where the mushrooms are growing because the nutrients have been absorbed by the fungi.

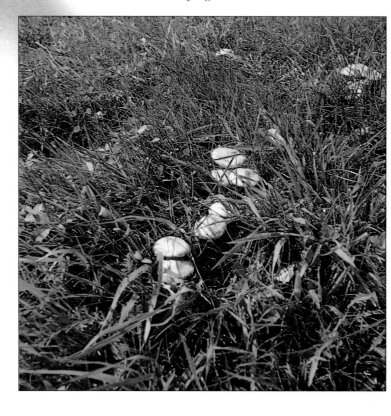

Morchella elata
BLACK MOREL

Another member of the highly edible morel family. This, like *Morchella esculenta*, grows in the early spring, so keep an eye open for it as soon as spring arrives.

IDENTIFICATION
Morchella elata is very similar to *M. esculenta* but much darker, often almost black with the ridges and pits aligned in vertical rows. The cap is often tall and pointed. The mushroom stands 5–15 cm (2–6 in) high.

HABITAT AND SEASON
Grows in gardens, wasteland, along roadsides and disused railway lines. Season is throughout the spring.

STORAGE
Like *M. esculenta*, the black morel is best dried.

PREPARATION AND
COOKING HINTS
Clean thoroughly before cooking, slicing the fruit body in half to ensure it is free of woodlice and so on. Cook and serve as you would *M. esculenta* and, like that morel, it must be properly cooked before it is eaten.

completely hollow cap

BELOW LEFT AND RIGHT *Another similar morel is the common morel,* Morchella vulgaris. *Look closely at these two examples, their caps may be dark but they have completely irregular pits and ridges unlike the black morels.*

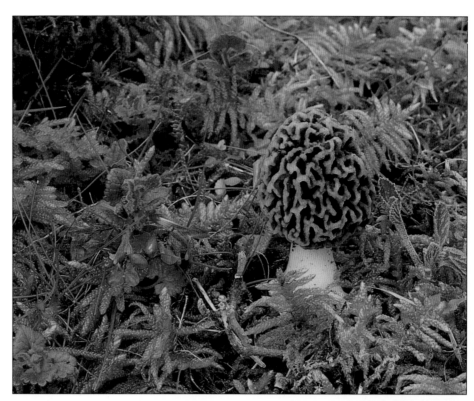

RIGHT *Often occuring in large numbers, the black morel may be found in both deciduous and coniferous woodlands as well as along tracks and in gardens.*

Morchella esculenta

The morels are among the most exciting springtime fungi. Careful examination of their habitat is necessary because they blend into their background so well. They usually grow singly; two or three can sometimes be found within a reasonably small area, but very rarely more. Excellent mushrooms from the culinary point of view, they must be cooked before eating – never, ever, eat them raw.

IDENTIFICATION
The fruit body is 5–20 cm (2–7¾ in) high. Although very convoluted, with a honeycomb effect, the overall shape is pointed. It is palish brown in colour and darkens to orange-yellow with age. Inside it is hollow. The flesh is white to cream.

HABITAT AND SEASON
Found among shrubs or in open woodland, on waste ground, along path edges and often along disused railway lines. The season is throughout the spring. Wind is very important in spreading the spore of this fungus so, if you find a good specimen, follow the direction of the prevailing wind and you will often find some more.

STORAGE
Best dried for storage. Because of all the nooks and crannies, this morel is often infested with woodlice and other wildlife, so specimens will need cleaning very thoroughly before drying and storing.

PREPARATION AND COOKING HINTS
The easiest way to clean this mushroom properly is to slice each one in half to make sure there is nothing hiding inside, rinse it in clear water and dry. One of the nicest ways to use fresh morels is to stuff the large fruit body. They also go well with meat dishes and provide a very rich sauce. Dried, the intensity of their flavour will enhance most dishes.

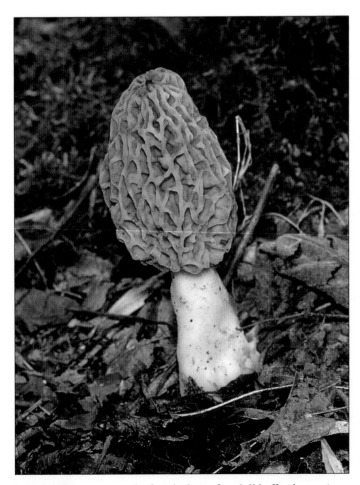

ABOVE *When young, the fruit body is often dull buff or brown in colour with blunt ridges.*

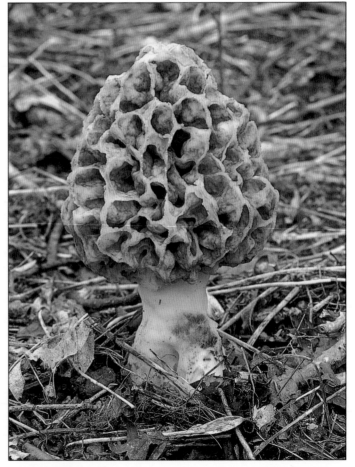

ABOVE *When mature, the colour changes to ochre or orange-yellow and the ridges become sharper.*

old caps are
quite yellow

completely
hollow
cap and stem

cap joins
stem without
overhang

stem base often
very swollen

pits and ridges
are very irregular,
never in vertical
lines as in the
black morel

young caps
very dark

Pleurotus cornucopiae

BELOW *The stems here are shorter than usual for they often reach 5–8 cm (2–3 in) in length. The way that the stems are fused together is quite characteristic.*

This member of the oyster mushroom family is fairly widely spread. It can be found on the same trees and at the same time as the oyster mushroom, so always have a good look for it before you leave the tree.

IDENTIFICATION

The cap is 5–12 (2–4¾ in) across and convex. It often makes quite a funnel-like shape, which frequently becomes fluted and split at the edges. Whitish in colour, almost a magnolia shade, it turns a fairly dark brown with age. The stem is 5–8 cm (2–3 in). Several fans may grow from the same stem, rather like flowers. The gills are quite deep and run down the stem; they are white to light tan in colour. The flesh is white and has a rather mealy smell. The spore print is lilac.

HABITAT AND SEASON

It grows in dense clusters on cut stumps of most deciduous trees, in particular elm, oak and beech. The season is spring to late autumn.

STORAGE

This mushroom air-dries well.

PREPARATION AND COOKING HINTS

If picked carefully, only a light wipe of the cap should be necessary. Discard most of the stalk as it will be quite tough, particularly where it was attached to the tree. The pleasant flavour makes it a good addition to all mushroom dishes.

gills run down the stem

often deep funnel-like cap

Pleurotus ostreatus
OYSTER MUSHROOM

BELOW *This is the grey-brown late-autumn/winter form of* Pleurotus ostreatus. *In summer, the cream-coloured form,* P. pulmonarius, *is common.*

Now grown commercially on a fairly large scale and so quite familiar, it is still exciting to find a wild oyster mushroom. They grow on dead or decaying trees, often in large masses. They will grow in the same place in successive years, so remember where you picked them.

IDENTIFICATION
The cap is 6–12 cm (2½–4¾ in) across. It is shaped rather like a fan and larger specimens may have fluted edges. The colour can vary: usually a slate grey, they can sometimes have a slightly brown or bluish tinge. They have almost no stem. The gills run down the stem; pure white at first, they turn cream with age. The flesh is white with a pleasant smell. The spore print is lilac. Oyster mushrooms grow in groups, one on top of the other, and if carefully removed from the tree are usually very clean.

HABITAT AND SEASON
These occur in large clusters on standing trees or on the stumps of fallen trees. Most commonly found

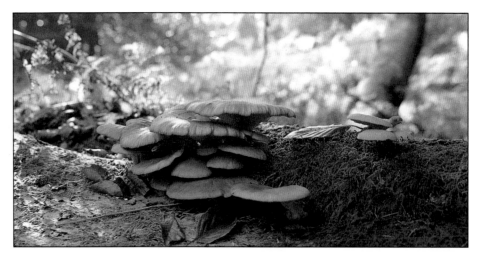

on beech trees, they will grow on other trees, especially elm. The season is all year round.

STORAGE
All methods of storage can be used for oyster mushrooms. If you separate the caps you can air-dry them very successfully.

PREPARATION AND COOKING HINTS
If picked carefully they are likely to be clean and a wipe with a damp cloth is probably all they need. The oyster mushroom's pleasant flavour means that it goes well with almost all meats and fish, making it extremely useful in the kitchen.

stems may be absent

crowded gills run down the stem

Russula cyanoxantha
CHARCOAL BURNER

The charcoal burner is an excellent mushroom to eat. However, it is a member of a very large genus and identification within the group can be very difficult. Correct identification is essential because some are poisonous, in particular the beechwood sickener, *Russula mairei*, and the sickener, *Russula emetica*. As always, if in doubt leave it out.

IDENTIFICATION
The cap is 5–18 cm (2–7 in) across and slightly greasy. Convex at first, it opens out with a shallow depression in the centre. Occasionally a single colour but more often than not quite a mixed shade, ranging from purple to light green, frequently with a rather faded appearance. The stem is 5–10 cm (2–4 in) and white. The gills run down the stem and are whitish or pale cream in older specimens. A clear identification feature of the charcoal burner is that the gills do not break away if they are touched, they are quite clearly joined to the cap margin. This is in marked contrast to some *Russula* species. The flesh is white and the smell is pleasant. The spore print is white.

HABITAT AND SEASON
Usually to be found under broad-leaved trees, but can also grow in association with pine trees. The season is summer to late autumn and it can be very common.

STORAGE
Drying is a very good method of storing the charcoal burner.

PREPARATION AND COOKING HINTS
It is rare to find a perfect specimen, as woodland wildlife attack it from almost the moment it appears. As a result it will need careful cleaning. However, it is good to eat whether fresh or dried and will add an interesting taste and texture to your mushroom dishes as it retains quite a crunchy texture when cooked. But do remember to be careful with your identification of the charcoal burner and make sure it is not one of the poisonous *Russula* species.

cap is often of mixed colours or even green

stem is white, sometimes flushed lavender

crowded white gills

RIGHT AND BELOW *The dull violet-purple cap shown here is typical, but beware, the cap can also be completely green. The best means of identification is to brush your fingers over the gills and they should be flexible and not crumbly as most other Russulas are.*

BELOW *A large and colourful group of mushrooms, all Russula species. The mushrooms in this family are some of the most difficult to identify accurately.*

Sparassis crispa
CAULIFLOWER FUNGUS

The cauliflower fungus is quite unlike any other fungus you will find in the woods. When you find one you will understand why it got its name. It is quite unusual, but grows in the same place year after year, so make a note of where you find it. One large specimen can last for several days if stored carefully in a cool place with its base in water.

IDENTIFICATION
The cauliflower fungus has no cap in the ordinary sense of the word, instead the fruit body is built up of many layers that resemble a cauliflower or a brain. A short stem attaches it to the tree on which it grows. The fruit body ranges from 20–50 cm (7¾–19¾ in) in diameter. It ages from a pale yellow-white to brown. It has a sweet smell and a lovely nutty flavour.

HABITAT AND SEASON
It grows on the roots of pine trees, very close to the trunks. Be careful not to cut too deeply when picking this fungus so as not to destroy the main mycelial growth from the roots, then you will be able to come back for more in subsequent seasons.

Look out for *Sparassis vipes*, a subspecies of *S. crispa*. This lives on old oak stumps as well as pine trees and is slightly pinkish. Please do not pick this one, it is very rare and is best left where it is to protect a fragile species.

The cauliflower fungus grows from late summer to late autumn but is tender to frosts and so will be killed by the first hard frosts of winter.

STORAGE
This dries extremely well. Air-drying is probably best: hang your specimens up on strings in a light, airy place for several days. Very large specimens can be cut into sections so they will dry more quickly. As the fungi dry the wildlife in them will fall out, so do not attempt to dry them in

colour varies from buff to creamy white

D
I
B
L
E

M
U
S
H
R
O
O
M
S

LEFT *Note the flattened crispy lobes. If they are pointed and branched you have probably mistakenly picked one of the* Ramaria *species which are often toxic.*

your kitchen; an airy shed or outside storeroom would be best. Any hint of dampness will, of course, spoil the drying. It is very important to dry this mushroom thoroughly – be patient, it will be worth it.

RIGHT *The fruit bodies are almost always at the base of a tree or stump, as seen here.*

PREPARATION AND COOKING HINTS

Pick only creamy white specimens, as this is when the fungus will be at its very best. Cleaning needs care as there are so many nooks and crannies in the cauliflower fungus and, as it grows so close to the ground pine needles can be a problem. If possible avoid cleaning in water. It is better to brush away any dust particles, cut into thin slices and clean each slice before cooking. If you do use water, remember to dry the fungus well on kitchen paper before cooking. One of the nicest ways to deal with this fungus is to cut it in thin slices, dip them in a batter made with beer rather than milk and deep-fry to make a wonderfully crisp nutty starter to a meal or accompaniment to a favourite dish. But it is equally good if sliced fresh and added to stews and casseroles.

edges of lobes turn brown with age

89

Suillus luteus (syn. *Boletus luteus*)

SLIPPERY JACK, PINE BOLETE OR STICKY BUN

The slippery jack is quite common and a good find, although its open texture makes it prone to maggot infestation. Much prized by chefs, it is very versatile in the kitchen.

IDENTIFICATION
The cap is 5–15 cm (2–6 in) across; a nice mid-brown colour with a marked sheen. It tends to be very sticky when wet, so is best picked in dry conditions. The stem is 5–10 cm (2–4 in), pale yellow with a large, clearly visible ring. The pores are pale yellow. The flesh is white. It has no particularly distinctive smell. The spore print is light brown. Only pick mature fresh specimens.

HABITAT AND SEASON
Found in association with conifers, particularly Scots pine. The season is late summer to late autumn.

STORAGE
Because of its soft texture, this mushroom is best thinly sliced and dried for use in winter dishes.

slimy surface when moist

pores unchanged by bruising

thick purple ring

PREPARATION AND COOKING HINTS

As the cap is slightly sticky in texture it is best peeled before use. Check carefully for maggot infestation. This mushroom exudes quite a lot of juice when cooking, so it is a good idea to sweat it out first on its own. Strain well and keep the resulting liquid to be used later for a sauce. Then add the mushrooms to other dishes. Slippery jack can be used in many ways. One nice one is to mix the sweated mushrooms with rashers of grilled or fried streaky bacon, add the strained juice, thicken with a little flour and serve it on toast.

BELOW *This and other* Suillus *species are only found growing under conifers.*

BOTTOM *Observe how the cap colours change from young to old. The purple-brown turns pale to orange-brown with age.*

Suillus variegatus

Another useful bolete to add to your collection, although it is not as good to eat as the cep or the bay boletus. Only pick young specimens. They are quite light in texture and therefore can become maggot-infested, so check specimens before collecting.

IDENTIFICATION
The cap is 5–12 cm (2–4¾ in) across and a rusty colour. It is sticky when wet. The stem is 5–9 cm (2–3½ in). The pores are quite clearly a snuff-brown colour. The flesh is very white. The spore print is light brown.

HABITAT AND SEASON
Found almost exclusively with conifers. The season is from late summer to late autumn.

STORAGE
Best dried.

dry, slightly
felted, scaly surface

PREPARATION AND COOKING HINTS
A wipe of the cap is usually all that is necessary, but beware when slicing specimens to look out for maggot infestation. A good addition to mixed mushroom dishes.

white flesh
sometimes stains
faintly blue

dark pores
with smaller
pores within the
larger are very
characteristic

Tricholoma ponderosa

WHITE MATSUTAKE

BELOW *This large species has a single layered ring at the stem apex, some lookalike larger species will have double rings at the top.*

This is one of the larger mushrooms and is much favoured by the Japanese. It is excellent whether eaten fresh or dried.

IDENTIFICATION

The cap is 4–25 cm (1½–9¾ in) across, convex becoming flat, with a broken margin. It is slightly inrolled at first, but opens fully with age. It has a smooth surface which feels quite tacky when dry. It is pale white and can be streaked with light brown. The stem can be up to 15 cm (6 in); it is solid and is sheathed with a veil that runs from the cap to the base. It breaks in patches and can become pinkish-brown, and quite fibrous around the root. The gills are white, attached and crowded. The white flesh, which can stain light brown, has a slightly spicy smell. The spore print is white.

HABITAT AND SEASON

It is scattered in coastal areas in sandy soil and is usually found in conjunction with conifers. Not known to grow in Europe, it is common in North America. The season is late summer to mid-autumn.

STORAGE

Drying is the best method of storage.

Whole mushrooms can be dried quite easily, using an electric dryer, by hanging them up or by placing them on drying racks. Dried ones can often be found in Japanese and Chinese supermarkets.

PREPARATION AND COOKING HINTS

Likely to be clean when you find it, it will need little more than washing. It adds an interesting flavour to wild mushroom dishes, but is quite strident, so be careful what you use it with and how much you use. As it has a large cap, it can also be used for stuffed mushroom dishes.

Tuber aestivum
SUMMER TRUFFLE

Although summer truffles grow far more extensively than most people realize, finding them is difficult for they grow beneath the surface of the soil. Animals love them, particularly squirrels and deer, so watching them might give you a clue as to where to look.

IDENTIFICATION
The fruit body is 2–10 cm (¾–4 in) across. It is irregular, though roughly globe-shaped, and covered in a host of tiny black warts. It is blackish-brown in colour. When cut through, it reveals a wonderfully marbled, reddish-brown interior. The smell is very distinctive and sweet and the taste is nutty.

HABITAT AND SEASON
The summer truffle favours cal-careous soils and can be found in the ground near beech trees, and also, though less often, in association with sweet chestnuts and evergreen oaks. The season is from late summer to autumn.

STORAGE
One of the best ways of storing truffles is preserving them in olive oil. First of all clean the truffle care-fully and shave off the skin which can be used in future recipes. Blanch the truffles very quickly before placing in oil in a completely air-tight container.

PREPARATION AND
COOKING HINTS
As truffles have a very strong flavour they are best used in small amounts and even a tiny quantity can trans-form a dish. They are delicious served with egg and pasta dishes.

spores are dispersed by burrowing animals and insects

Tuber magnatum
THE PIEDMONT OR WHITE TRUFFLE

This must be the prize for all mushroom hunters. The most sought-after of the truffles, it is found in very limited areas, mostly in northern Italy, where the finest certainly grow. Unfortunately highly trained dogs or pigs are necessary to locate it.

IDENTIFICATION
The fruit body is generally 5–12 cm (2–4¾ in) across, although much larger, tennis-ball-sized specimens do occasionally occur. It is irregular in shape and yellowish-brown in colour. Indeed, in colour and size it is not unlike a new potato. The flesh is marbled and has a slightly reddish-brown tinge. The smell is highly distinctive and very sweet.

HABITAT AND SEASON
Just below the soil surface in mossy mixed woodlands. Its season is from late autumn through the winter to early spring. Due to its intense smell, it is found usually by dogs or pigs.

STORAGE
These truffles are best stored in closed containers and used fairly quickly after collecting. They have an intense flavour which can permeate foods, so use them to flavour eggs before cooking. Alternatively, put in a closed container with freshly made pasta and leave in the fridge overnight. This gives the pasta a most wonderful truffle scent. The best method of storage would definitely be in extra virgin olive oil. It will not only preserve the truffle but will flavour the oil and give it a wonderfully rich truffle taste. These are the most valued of the wild fungi and command extremely high prices. Excellent quality ones can be obtained from specialist importers and the truffle oil, the fresh truffles or the truffles in extra virgin oil are well worth buying.

PREPARATION AND COOKING HINTS
Very little needs doing to the truffle beyond a careful brushing. If they are to be used fresh, very finely sliced slivers, quickly cooked, are best for the intensity of the flavour. They can also be eaten raw.

solid marbled flesh has strong odour

smooth but lumpy surface is characteristic

Poisonous Mushrooms

INTRODUCTION

Every year, in spite of repeated warnings, people die of mushroom poisoning. Such deaths emphasize the importance of identifying your mushrooms correctly. People often make the literally fatal mistake of assuming that if animals can eat a mushroom so can humans. Unfortunately this is untrue, for example, slugs eat death caps and other members of the genus *Amanita*. So do not be mistaken when you see signs of either bird or animal activity; it is probably safe for them but may not be for you. Be particularly careful if dealing with the *Amanitas*, remember that their spores are poisonous and that if eaten they will cause extensive damage to the liver and central nervous system. If you think you are dealing with an *Amanita*, dig out the whole specimen with a stick to examine the volval bag. It is a good idea to protect your hand with a glove.

Never, ever, put a poisonous mushroom or an unidentified one with others in your basket. If you require a specimen for identification, put it in a separate container, and always wash your hands after touching any unidentified mushrooms. If you pick a deadly *Amanita* for display, throw the mushroom and container immediately after use. A good way to transport and display such mushrooms is to put them in a plastic container on crumpled paper and to cover the whole box with clingfilm. People can then see the mushroom without having to touch it. There are many old wives' tales about how to identify edible and poisonous mushrooms. They are all false. Particularly dangerous is the saying that if you can peel it you can eat it. You can peel a death cap, which got its name for a very good reason! Other sayings refer to staining silver spoons black. Ignore them all, and take great care over identification so that you can be sure of living to enjoy your mushroom trophies.

Between the good edible mushrooms and the deadly poisonous ones, there is an enormous range of other mushrooms regarded as inedible or not worthwhile. These are not all included in this book. Should you require information about them, consult one of the guides listed at the end of this book.

Although most people can eat the edible mushrooms and fungi identified in this book, it is important to remember that eating large quantities of a very rich food can often cause upset stomachs and some people do have an adverse reaction to fungi. Among those that could cause problems are the wood blewit, *Lepista nuda*, and the field blewit, *Lepista saeva*. Should you ever become ill after eating mushrooms, it is important to see your doctor immediately. Mushroom poisoning can occur almost instantaneously or up to fourteen hours after eating the mushrooms, and at any time in between. It is imperative that you seek medical advice and, if possible, take a sample of the mushroom you have eaten. Correct identification of the poison could be life-saving, and there are many cases of *Amanita* poisoning being dealt with early enough to save the victim's life.

Another mushroom to beware of is the yellow stainer, *Agaricus xanthodermus*. A member of the genus *Agaricus*, it grows in similar situations to the ordinary field or horse mushroom and can be quite common in good mushroom years. Safety is the key for all collectors, so if you are not sure about a mushroom, leave it out of your basket.

PREVIOUS PAGE *A typical group of fly agarics,* Amanita muscaria, *showing how the red pigment fades at the edges with age or after rain.*

LEFT *The* Clitocybe rivulosa, *similar to the fairy champignon but highly toxic.*

OPPOSITE *The death cap,* Amanita phalloides. *The slight radial streaking on the cap can be seen well here.*

Agaricus xanthodermus

YELLOW STAINER OR YELLOW-STAINING MUSHROOM

The yellow stainer accounts for approximately 50 per cent of the cases of mushroom poisoning among those who pick either field or horse mushrooms. It has an unpleasant smell and taste and must be avoided at all costs. Identification can be difficult and therefore take careful note of the identification features and illustrations. The symptoms of poisoning are sweating and flushing with unpleasant stomach cramps. Not everyone is affected by the yellow stainer, but it is not worth taking any risks – leave it well alone.

IDENTIFICATION

The cap is 5–15 cm (2–6 in) across. Convex and angular at first, it flattens out later with a dip in the centre.

intense yellow stains on surface when scratched

cap becomes greyish and slightly scaly with age

mature gills turn brown

LEFT *Gardens, hedgerows and the edges of woodland are favourite habitats of this species.*

thick ring joins cap to stem

Very white when young, it darkens with age as it expands to a fairly large cap with greyish-brown scales. It bruises a very bright yellow as soon as it is touched or cut, making this a valuable identification feature. Although this mushroom has many similarities with other members of the agaric family, the bright yellow staining is the giveaway. The stem is 5–15 cm (2–6 in) and white, staining bright yellow at the base. The gills are flesh-coloured, darkening with age. The flesh is white. Smell is an important means of identifying this mushroom as it smells rather of carbolic. The spore print is purple-brown. Should you have picked a yellow stainer by mistake and put it in your pan it will quite often turn the rest of the contents a slimy sickly yellow. It will also give off an acrid smell in the kitchen that is very unpleasant.

HABITAT AND SEASON
It grows in woods, pastures and gardens. It has quite a long season, from summer to late autumn. It is quite common in certain areas.

Amanita citrina and *Amanita citrina* var. *alba*

FALSE DEATH CAP

There are two forms of the false death cap, *Amanita citrina* and *Amanita citrina* var. *alba*. Although neither are deadly poisonous, they are so easily confused with the death cap that it is best to leave them alone.

IDENTIFICATION

There are two distinct forms of this fungi: one with a pale greenish-yellow tinge to the cap (*A. citrina*) and the other with a pure white cap. (*A. citrina* var. *alba*). In both forms the cap is 4–10 cm (1½–4 in) across. It is usually covered with patches of the veil, which is one of the features that distinguishes it from the death cap which rarely has any veil remnants. The stem is 6–8 cm (2½–3 in). It has a large basal bag where the remnants of the veil can be seen and it has a clear ring around the stem. The gills are off-white at first, darkening with age. The flesh is white. The spore print is white.

HABITAT AND SEASON

Grows in deciduous or coniferous woods, especially beech woods, but can be found in a large variety of locations. The season is from summer to late autumn and it is quite common.

RIGHT *The false death cap grows in both coniferous and deciduous woodlands. A pure white form is common under beech. A potato-like smell is typical.*

veil fragments mostly washed

BELOW *In this example, the prominent flat white patches of veil have washed off the cap leaving it quite smooth.*

bulb with gutter-like margin

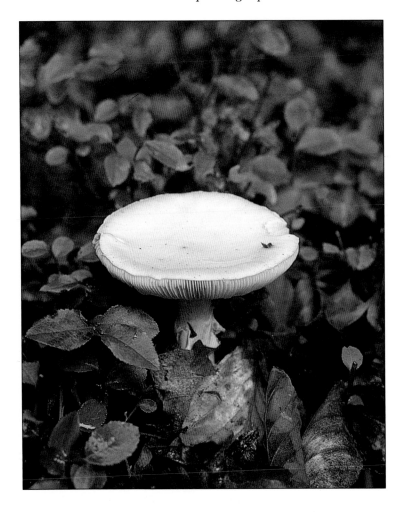

Amanita muscaria
FLY AGARIC

Without doubt this is everybody's idea of a toadstool or poisonous mushroom. The little flecks on the red cap which sometimes grows to 20 cm (7¾ in) across make it quite distinctive. Many fables of myth and magic are associated with this mushroom. One, which sounds like a myth but is not, is its use by the Sami people of Lapland to round up their reindeer herds. They take advantage of the reindeers' liking for the fly agaric and scatter dried ones for the reindeer to eat, which makes them more manageable. The toxins contained in *Amanita muscaria* attack the central nervous system producing intoxication, hallucination and a euphoria that is similar to drunkenness. The poison stays in the system for several months but the symptoms generally disappear in twelve hours, although it may take several days to fully recover.

The only mushroom you are likely to mistake for *A. muscaria* is *A. caesarea*. However, *A. caesarea* has a large volval bag whereas *A. muscaria* does not. In addition, when cut lengthways, *A. muscaria* is white whereas *A. caesarea* is yellow. Another pointer is that the cap of *A. caesarea* does not show flecks of the remnants of the volval bag. When the volval bag finally breaks, it leaves *A. caesarea* clean. *A. caesarea* grows in limited locations throughout Europe except the United Kingdom.

IDENTIFICATION

The cap of the fly agaric is 8–20 cm (3–7¾ in) across, cup-shaped at first, it then flattens right out. Although usually bright scarlet and covered with flecks of veil remnant, the colour may fade in wet weather, and a

remains of veil

white gills do not join the stem

few come up a fairly pale orange. The white stem is 8–18 cm (3–7 in). If you take a specimen right out of the ground you will see the rounded, swollen stem base. (The gills are white.) The smell is indistinct. These often occur in fairly large groups at all stages of development. The spore print is white.

HABITAT AND SEASON

The fly agaric is most often found with birch trees, although it can occur with a wide range of trees and in many locations. The season is late summer to late autumn and it is very common.

BELOW *This is the Caesar's mushroom. Unlike the fly agaric, the cap on Caesar's mushroom is clean.*

BOTTOM *After heavy rain the flecks may wash off the cap and the red colour fade to orange.*

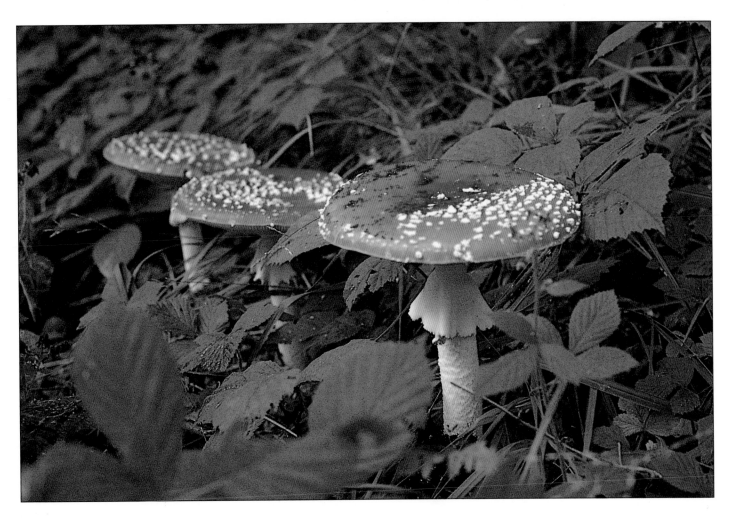

Amanita pantherina
PANTHER CAP

Less common than the fly agaric, the panther cap, *Amanita pantherina*, too, is severely toxic. The greatest danger with the panther cap is that it can be confused with the blusher, *Amanita rubescens*. Many people eat the blusher after first cooking it to remove the toxins and then using it normally. However, it requires a very expert eye to distinguish between young specimens of the blusher and the panther cap, so it is best to avoid both species for fear of making a mistake.

IDENTIFICATION
The cap is 5–10 cm (2–4 in) across, almost bronze in colour, and covered with small pure white remnants of veil. The margin also has remnants of the veil. The stem is 9–12.5 cm (3½–5 in), white with a ring. It has a very bulbous base and narrow ring, very

narrow, hoop-like ring low down on stem

pure white fragments of universal veil

one or more rings of tissue around bulb-like base

low down which forms a distinct free rim around the base. There are usually also one or two belted rings immediately above the bulb. The spore print is white.

HABITAT AND SEASON

The panther cap is very uncommon, growing with both coniferous and deciduous trees. The season is mid-summer to late autumn.

ABOVE *Beech woods on limestone soils are the favourite habitat of the panther cap although it will grow under conifers as well.*

RIGHT *This picture illustrates the narrow hoop-like ring around the middle of the stem.*

Amanita phalloides
DEATH CAP

Each year the death cap accounts for most of the fatal poisonings caused by eating mushrooms. It looks fairly innocuous, smells pleasant and can be peeled. However, it is deadly and only one cap is needed to cause serious, possibly fatal, poisoning. The range of colours can be quite dramatic, making identification even more difficult. It can vary from a sickly green to dark brown to pale white, so great care must be taken over identification. If you go on a foray, make sure the foray leader finds one to point out to you. If it is dug out of the ground you will see the volval bag at the base very clearly. Take a good look and remember what you see, for a large specimen can kill several people.

IDENTIFICATION

The cap is 3–15 cm (1¼–6 in) across. It is quite round at first, flattening with age. It has a smooth, almost shiny surface. The colour is quite often greenish turning to a rather dirty brown, but beware, in wet weather the cap can become quite light. The stem is 5–12.5 cm (2–5 in) and white. The gills are free and quite crowded; white at first, mature specimens may have an almost flesh-coloured tinge. The flesh is white with a yellow tinge by the cap, and it smells quite sweet. The volval sac or bag is quite pronounced. The spore print is white.

HABITAT AND SEASON

Widespread in mixed deciduous woodland, particularly in association with oak. The season is early summer to quite late autumn.

The death cap deserves its name, it is the most deadly fungus known to

white unchanging gills

olive cap may sometimes be white or yellowish

white, bag-like volva surrounds stem base

RIGHT *The caps often have a slightly radially streaked or fibrous appearance.*

mankind and years of research have not produced any antidote to the poison. Many have tried and some people have been saved by having their blood screened through charcoal, once the hospital had identified it as *Amanita* poisoning. The symptoms of poisoning take between 10 and 24 hours to become apparent, but during that time the poison has been attacking the liver and the kidneys. The first signs of poisoning are prolonged sickness and diarrhoea with severe abdominal pains; this is often followed by a period of apparent recovery when all seems well. However, death from liver and kidney failure will occur within a few days. There is a rare form of *A. phalloides* which is *A. phalloides* var. *alba*. Apart from being pure white throughout, which makes it look deceptively like an innocent mushroom, the features by which you will identify it are exactly the same and it is just as deadly.

ABOVE *The volva at the stem base may be completely hidden under the leaf litter, as seen here – beware!*

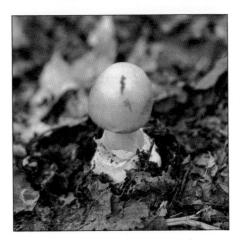

LEFT *Always carefully clear away around the stem base to expose the remains of a volva.*

Amanita virosa
DESTROYING ANGEL

Like many *Amanitas*, the destroying angel grows from a volval bag. It is deadly poisonous and well deserves its name, being white and fatal. The symptoms of the poison are the same as for *Amanita phalloides*.

IDENTIFICATION
The cap is 5–15 cm (2–6 in) across, bell-shaped at first, it becomes very irregular when open. It is pure white. The stem is 9–12 cm (3½–4¾ in) and grows from a fairly large volval bag that is not regular at the base, but can clearly be seen with the fungus growing from it. There is a white ring which is very fragile and often incomplete. The gills are pure white. The flesh is white and the smell is slightly sickly. The spore print is white.

HABITAT AND SEASON
Grows in mixed deciduous woodland and is happily not as common as the death cap. The season is usually midsummer to autumn. If you are on a foray, this is another mushroom that you should ask the foray leader to point out to you, for once seen you will be unlikely to forget it.

slightly pointed cap

large, white bag-like volva

RIGHT *The cap of this species often has a distinct hump or blunt point at the centre.*

Clitocybe dealbata

Do not be fooled by this innocent-looking little mushroom, it is severely toxic. It often grows in just the places that many edible mushrooms grow.

IDENTIFICATION
The cap is 2–5 cm (¾–2 in) across, flat with a depression slightly inrolled and fluted round the edge. It is off-white in colour. The stem is 2–3 cm (¾–1¼ in) and whitish. The gills are quite crowded and run part way down the stem. They are almost and it has a mealy smell. The spore print is white.

HABITAT AND SEASON
Grows in lawns, pasturelands and old meadows, often in troops or rings. It can be also be found in open woodland. The season is summer to late autumn and it is quite common.

BELOW *This shows the rather frosted appearance of the white caps and the slightly decurrent gills.*

gills run down the stem (decurrent)

silky or frosted appearance of cap surface

Clitocybe rivulosa

BELOW *The* Clitocybe rivulosa *mushrooms are usually a silky greyish-white, as here.*

Another innocent-looking, but severely toxic mushroom that can easily be confused with the edible fairy ring champignon, *Marasmius oreades*. Both grow in rings, in similar situations and at much the same time of the year. Indeed it is not uncommon for rings of each species to grow within a few metres of each other. So take care. It would probably be a good idea to seek out live examples of both before you start picking the fairy ring champignon.

smooth silky cap

although the gills are buff the spores are white.

gills run down the stem

slightly funnel-shaped cap

gills are crowded

HABITAT AND SEASON
In troops or rings in sandy soil amongst grass, beside paths and roads. The season is late summer to late autumn and it is very common.

BELOW *These caps are rather waterlogged and so appear browner than normal. Usually they are a silky greyish-white.*

IDENTIFICATION
The cap is 2–5 cm (¾–2 in) across; cup-shaped at first, it soon flattens out with a small depression in the centre. The margin remains slightly rolled. It is grey and concentric rings are visible. The stem is 2–4 cm (¾–1½ in) and a similar colour to the cap. The crowded, grey gills run part way down the stem. The flesh is dirty white to grey. The closeness of the gills and the colour and shape of the cap are important ways to distinguish this mushroom from the fairy ring champignon. The spore print is white.

Coprinus atramentarius
COMMON INK CAP

The common ink cap is not poisonous in itself, but if eaten in conjunction with alcohol, it can cause alarming symptoms, such as nausea, palpitations and stomach cramps. For this reason it has been used over the years in attempts to cure alcoholics. The ink cap gets its name from the fact that it was used many years ago by monks to produce an exceptionally fine drawing ink, made by boiling the collapsed inky caps with a little water and a hint of cloves. The difference between the common ink cap and the shaggy ink cap is quite marked, but it is important that you recognize this one for it would be a catastrophe to make a mistake at a dinner party at which you were serving alcohol. Young specimens of the magpie fungus, *Coprinus picaceus*, could be confused with the common ink cap. Although not as common as this, it grows in fairly large quantities in the late summer to autumn. It is best avoided because although not poisonous it can cause nausea and vomiting in some people.

IDENTIFICATION

The cap is 2–4 cm (¾–1½ in) across, white and bell-shaped. Light grey to greyish-brown in colour, with veil remnants often attached to the cap. The stem is 7–17 cm (2¾–6¾ in) and white. The gills are crowded, white at first, they change from brown to a dark inky mass. The smell is not distinctive. The spore print is brown.

HABITAT AND SEASON

The common ink cap grows in tufts, often in association with buried wood. The season is from spring to late autumn and they are very common, often growing in large troops.

gills blacken
and liquify when
mature from the
edge inwards

note brown
scaly base
to stem

LEFT *This is one
of the most common
species in towns,
gardens and
woodlands
everywhere,
often associated
with dead or
buried wood.*

Galerina autumnalis
DEADLY GALERINA

This fungus is deadly poisonous and must be avoided. The poisoning is very similar to the effects of the *Amanita* family.

IDENTIFICATION
The cap is 2.5–7 cm (1–2¾ in) across. It is convex at first, becoming flat with a slight dome at the centre. It is a dark brown fading to a light buff with age, and when moist is quite sticky and shiny. The hollow stem is 2–10 cm (¾–4 in) and fairly bulbous at the base. There are slight brownish to blackish markings at the base of the stem, and the mycelial threads are clearly visible at the bottom. There is a veil that breaks fairly easily and is quite small. The gills are attached and quite close, yellowish in colour, becoming redder with age. The flesh is off-white. The deadly galerina has no distinct smell. The spore print is dull orange-brown.

HABITAT AND SEASON
The deadly galerina tends to live on well-decayed coniferous or deciduous wood, often in quite large troops. Its season is from late spring to autumn. The deadly galerina is not known in Europe, but quite common in North America. The very similar *G. marginata*, however, is quite common in Britain and is equally deadly.

ABOVE *Note the brownish-yellow gills which distinguish this from edible species such as the honey fungus.*

Hygrophoropsis aurantiaca
FALSE CHANTERELLE

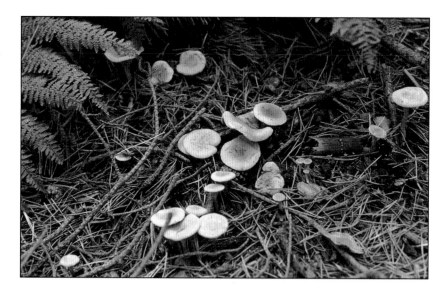

Although not poisonous in the way that agaric and amanita mushrooms are, the false chanterelle is known to cause gastro-intestinal problems.

IDENTIFICATION

The cap is 2–8 cm (¾–3 in) across, flat at first with a slightly inrolled margin, it becomes more funnel-shaped with age. In large specimens the cap is more fluted and looks much more like a chanterelle. However, the false chanterelle's cap is orange rather than the yellow of the true chanterelle. The gills are dark orange, close and run down the stem. The spore print is white.

ABOVE AND RIGHT *The false chanterelle is very common under both pines and birch trees, and the cap becomes funnel-shaped with age.*

crowded gills are soft and often forked

cap margin inrolled when young

HABITAT AND SEASON

Grows in coniferous woodland and on heathland. It is very common and often grows in troops close to chanterelles. The season is from summer to late autumn.

Hypholoma fasciculare
SULPHUR TUFT

This is a very common mushroom and grows all the year round, even in the winter. It is not deadly poisonous, but definitely should be avoided. It could be confused with other fungi, such as honey fungus *Armillaria mellea*, and brick cap, *Hyphoioma sublateritium*, that are extremely good to eat, so take care with your identification.

IDENTIFICATION

The cap is 2–9 cm (¾–3½ in) across and is convex. The remains of the yellow veil often adhere to the margin. The cap itself is bright yellow with a dark orange centre. The stem is 4–10 cm (1½–4 in), curved and a similar colour to the cap. The gills start bright yellow, but turn dark sulphur-green then brown with age. The flesh is bright yellow, becoming brownish near the base of the stem. It has quite a mushroomy smell. The spore print is purple-black.

HABITAT AND SEASON

This occurs in dense clusters on the rotting timber and stumps of deciduous and coniferous trees. It grows throughout the year.

note purple-brown
spores deposited
on stem

BELOW *One of the most common fungi everywhere on dead or dying wood, the sulphur tuft grows in large clumps.*

Inocybe patouillardii

RED-STAINING INOCYBE

The red-staining inocybe is severely toxic and therefore must not be eaten. Many of the others in this family are poisonous, if not as deadly as this one, therefore it is best to avoid all the inocybes.

IDENTIFICATION

The cap is 3–10 cm (1¼–4 in) across, slightly conical and uneven. The margins are often cracked, giving the typical appearance of an inocybe. Cream-coloured, the cap has red-staining fibres. The stem is 3–10 cm (1¼–4 in), fairly thick and slightly bulbous at the base. The gills are quite pink at first, like those of a mushroom, and then darken to a light brown colour. The flesh is white and has no particular smell. The spore print is dull brown.

HABITAT AND SEASON

Grows along paths in mixed woodland on chalky soils, especially those with beech and, less often, chestnut. The season is spring to late autumn.

RIGHT *The white fibrous cap and stem, with blood red stains when bruised, are very distinctive. The red-staining inocybe likes open woodlands on chalky soils.*

Lactarius pubescens

Lactarius pubescens is a member of the large milk cap family. It is important to be able to identify this mushroom for not only is it a strong emetic but it can be confused with the edible saffron milk cap (*Lactarius deliciosus*). The woolly edges of *Lactarius pubescens* are an important feature of identification.

IDENTIFICATION

The cap is 4–10 cm (1½–4 in) across, convex and slightly depressed with the margin markedly inrolled and woolly at the edge. It is often quite pale to rose pink; but this tends to fade in direct sunlight. The stem is 3–6 cm (1¼–2½ in) and a palish pink. The gills are crowded, light pink and tend to darken with age. They run down the stem. The flesh is quite thick and whitish, but can have a pinkish tinge. There is no particular smell. Equally common and shaggy

is *L. torminosus*, a brighter pink and equally upsetting if eaten.

HABITAT AND SEASON

This mushroom tends to grow fairly widely but often near birch trees on fairly poor or sandy soil. The season is from late summer through to quite late autumn.

*gills bleed
white milk
when cut*

*funnel-shaped
cap*

Paxillus involutus
BROWN ROLL-RIM

The brown roll-rim is a very common mushroom. It is also severely toxic. It can have a boletus-like shape, which makes matters worse, some boletus species being, of course, edible. The toxins have yet to be identified, but their effect is somewhat similar to leukaemia.

IDENTIFICATION
The cap size is 5–15 cm (2–6 in) across. It is quite flat when young, becoming convex and somewhat funnel-shaped with age. It gets its name from its clearly inrolled rim and mid- to red-brown colour. The cap is slippery when moist and shiny when dry. The stem is up to 7.5 cm (3 in) and similar in colour to the cap. The narrow, crowded gills are yellow turning brown to red-brown when bruised. The gills run down the stem. The spore print is sienna.

HABITAT AND SEASON
The brown roll-rim grows beside paths in broad-leaved woodland, especially with birch, and on quite acid heathland. It has a long growing season from summer to late autumn.

ABOVE *A mature cap with margin unrolled.*

ABOVE *This is an immature cap with tightly rolled cap margin.*

crowded gills bruise brown

inrolled margin

Russula emetica
THE SICKENER

There are at least 150 different species of *Russula*, making it one of the largest groups of fungi. Some, such as the charcoal burner, are edible, but many are highly poisonous. The sickener and the very similar looking beechwood sickener, *Russula mairei*, did not get their names without good reason. It is really best to leave this family very well alone.

IDENTIFICATION
The cap is 3–10 cm (1¼–4 in) across and is quite cup-shaped, later flattening with a shallow central depression. The cap is a brightish red, but sometimes has faded white areas.

When peeled, it shows red-coloured flesh underneath. The white stem is 4–9 cm (1½–3½ in). The gills are creamy, darkening slightly with age. The flesh is thin and fragile and can be quite sticky. It is white except under the cap. The smell is sweet and fruity. The spore print is whitish.

BELOW *The sickener is found under pines, especially in wet areas.*

HABITAT AND SEASON
Grows almost exclusively under pines. The season is summer to late autumn and it is very common. As its name suggests, the beechwood sickener, which has a similar season, grows almost exclusively under beech trees.

pure red cap skin peels off very easily

flesh is brittle and crumbly

widely spaced gills

GLOSSARY

asci The sacs in Ascomycetes in which the sexual spores are formed.

Acomycetes Group of fungi characterized by bearing the sexual spores in a sac (asci).

Basidiomycetes Group of fungi characterized by the presence of spore-bearing cells called basidia.

brackets Shelf-like fruit bodies.

cap The portion of the mushroom bearing the gills and the tubes.

convex A surface that is curved or rounded outwards.

decurrent Running down the stem.

fibrous Composed of fine fibres or threads.

flesh Inner tubes of a fungus.

fruit body Structure on which the spore-producing cells are held.

hymenium Layer of spore-producing cells.

inrolled Curled inwards and down.

marginate With a distinct ridge or gutter-like margin.

milk Sticky fluid released by some fungi when damaged.

network A mesh or pattern of criss-crossed fine ridges.

partial veil The fine web of tissue connecting the cap margin to the stem.

pores The openings of the clustered tubes in Boletes and Polypores.

recurved Curving backwards, i.e. scales with recurved tips.

ring Remains of the partial veil left on the stem.

scales Small to large raised flakes or flaps of tissue, usually on the cap or stem surface.

spore Reproductive cell of typical mushroom.

spore print A thick deposit of spores dropped by a mushroom cap onto paper.

stem The 'stalk' on which a mushroom cap is raised up.

striated With distinct parallel grooves or lines especially at the cap edge.

tubes The downward-pointing clusters of tubes on Boletes and Polypores within which the spores are produced.

universal veil The fine to thick covering of tissue which envelopes some fungi when immature.

volva Example of thick universal veil which remains as a bag at the base of the stem.

OPPOSITE *Horn of plenty*, Craterellus cornucopioides.

LEFT *Saffron milk-caps*, Lactarius deliciosus.

INDEX

Mushroom poisoning, 98

BIBLIOGRAPHY

ARORA, DAVID, *Mushrooms Demystified* (Berkeley 1986, 2nd ed)

STEVENSON, G., *Field Guide to Fungi* University of Canterbury Publication No. 30, Christchurch, New Zealand (Christchurch 1982)

CARLUCCIO, A., *A Passion for Mushrooms* (London 1989)

CLELAND, J.B., *Toadstools and Mushrooms and other Larger Fungi of South Australia* (Adelaide 1934, reprinted 1976)

DICKENSON, COLIN and LUCAS, JOHN, *The Encyclopedia of Mushrooms* (London 1979)

FINDLAY, W.P.K., *Wayside and Woodland Fungi* (London 1967)

FUHRER, B., *A Field Companion to Australian Fungi* (Victoria 1985)

GARNWEIDNER, E., *Mushrooms of Britain and Europe* (London 1994)

HURST, J. and RUTHERFORD, L., *A Gourmet's Book of Mushrooms and Truffles* (London 1991)

LINCOFF, GARY H., *The Audubon Society Field Guide to North American Mushrooms* (New York 1981)

LINCOFF, GARY H. and PARIONI, GIOVANNI ed., *Simon and Shuster's Guide to Mushrooms* (New York 1981)

KIBBY, G., *An Illustrated Guide to Mushrooms and Other Fungi of Britain and Northern Europe* (London 1982)

MACDONALD, R and WESTERMAN, J., *Fungi of South-eastern Australia* (Victoria 1979)

MILLER, ORSON K., *Mushrooms of North America* (New York 1978)

PHILLIPS, R., *Mushrooms and Other Fungi of Great Britain and Europe* (London 1981)

SHEPHERD, C.J. and TOTTERDELL, C.J., *Mushrooms and Toadstools of Australia* (Sydney 1988)

SMITH, ALEXANDER and WEBER, NANSY, S., *Mushroom Hunter's Field Guide* (Michigan 1980)

WOOD, A., *Australian Mushrooms and Toadstools – How to Identify Them* (Kensington 1980)

SOCIETIES

One of the best ways to learn about mushrooms is to go on a foray led by an expert. For details of local groups contact your library. Listed here are some of the main societies you might also like to write to for further information.

UNITED KINGDOM

British Mycological Society
c/o C.A.B. International
Mycological Institute
Ferry Lane
Kew
Surrey TW9 3AF

The Tasty Mushroom Partnership
Poppy Cottage
Station Road
Burnham Market
Norfolk PE31 8HA

BELOW *Horn of plenty*, Craterellus cornucopioides.

AUSTRALIA

Sydney Fungal Studies Group
50 Old Bells Line of Road
Kurrajong
NSW 2758

Australian Society for Microbiology
Unit 23
20 Commercial Road
Melbourne
Victoria 3004

ACKNOWLEDGEMENTS

The publishers and authors would like to thank the following people for their help in the production of this book: Geoffrey Kibby of the International Institute of Entomology, London; Andrew Broderick of the Australian Wild Fungi Research Group, School of Horticulture, University of Western Sydney, Hawkesbury, Bourke Street, Richmond NSW 2753 Australia; Clive Houlder, mushroom hunter and supplier of specialist fungi; L'aquila Products, 40 Caledonian Road, London, for providing the truffles; Valerie Jordan and Avril Henley for their help in typing the manuscript; Mycologue, 35 King Henry's Road, London, for providing the knives; Patricia Michelson, La Fromagerie, 30 Highbury Park, London N5 2AA, specialist food finder; Taste of the Wild, 65 Overstrand Mansions, Prince of Wales Drive, London SW11 4EX, suppliers of wild mushrooms.

Picture credits
t = top, b = bottom, l = left, r = right
Heather Angel page 103br
Timothy J. Baroni 111t, 111b
George Dickson 45t, 45b, 118
Geoffrey Kibby 67tl, 70t, 83, 81tl
George McCarthy 2, 6/7, 15b, 17t, 22/23, 24, 281, 28r, 29b, 34, 35b, 47b, 59t, 59b, 61t, 63m, 65b, 73t, 77b, 82tr, 82r, 96/97, 98, 106, 107l, 107r, 113b, 246
Gregory Mueller 31b, 61b, 63b, 66/67, 81b, 82l, 93, 115
Oxford Scientific Films (David Thompson) 29t; (G I Bernard) 30, 31t; (Jack Dermid) 105t

BELOW *Winter chanterelle,* Cantharellus infundibuliformis.